JANEZ BRATOVŽ
SLOVENIAN CUISINE

JANEZ BRATOVŽ

SLOVENIAN CUISINE
FROM THE ALPS TO THE
ADRIATIC IN 20 INGREDIENTS

SKYHORSE PUBLISHING

SLOVENIAN CUISINE

FROM THE ALPS TO THE ADRIATIC IN 20 INGREDIENTS

Recipes: JANEZ BRATOVŽ
Text: NOAH CHARNEY
Portrait photos: MATJAŽ TANČIČ
Food photos: MANCA JEVŠČEK
Design: ŽARE KERIN / FUTURA DDB
Typesetting: MARJAN BOŽIČ / FUTURA DDB
Translations: ALENKA BRATINA
Foreword: HIROSHI ISHIDA

DISHES FILLED WITH DREAMS AND KINDNESS

It is my great pleasure to write a foreword for Chef Janez Bratovž's new cookbook.

Janez first came to our restaurant, Mibu, in the summer of 2008. It was a surprise to me when he singled out one dish–blackened Kamo-nasu (eggplant). When he said that he was impressed with our dish, I immediately sensed that this chef must be on the same wavelength as I am. For this dish, the big and round Kamo-nasu eggplant, one of the traditional vegetables of Kyoto, was slowly roasted, without any spice, until its skin became blackened. By concentrating the eggplant juices and sweetness and adding a roasted aroma, umami develops and, at this tastiest moment, we serve the freshly-cooked hot eggplant to our guests. The eggplant, roasted without being cut, keeps its natural shape and looks so noble that it reminded me of the image of a meditating monk in a black gown that I venerated. Thus, the dish was named "Zazen nasu," or "meditation eggplant."

If we may describe Western cuisine as the art of flavoring, Japanese cuisine differs, and its essence is to appreciate the inherent characteristics of all sorts of food, such as vegetables and fish. Janez kindly expressed that he was impressed with the dish's sublime essence.

Soon after his visit, I had an opportunity to visit Slovenia. The dishes Janez created were filled with dreams and kindness, just as Janez is himself. The beauty of the food arranged on the plates in the dishes struck me. It felt like a prayer of his appreciation of the souls of each food and of modestly accepting them deep in his heart. I sympathized and, at the same time, I was attracted to his cuisine.

Both Slovenia and Japan have four seasons. The two countries enjoy wonderful products from the ocean, mountains, and fields, which have been appreciated and protected since long ago. Not only were we fortunate to have been born to these beautiful lands, with their abundant nature, but we have a fortunate destiny to deliver their blessing of food and harvest to others.

To a dear friend, congratulations, and I would like to share with you a teaching from a Zen nun whom I admire and always keep in mind while working: "In the rain and the wind, take your umbrella, but only open it 70% of the way. Whatever you may do, be careful not to extend it fully."

Hiroyoshi ISHIDA
Chef of MIBU Restaurant

CONTENTS

J B

━━━━━━

Little Janez lies in the high grasses beside a stream behind his grandmother's house in Trzin. His parents call to him. They are dressed in their finest clothes, just back from Germany where they have spent the last three years. Born in 1962, he has not seen them since they left in 1965, when he was three years old, and his brother was two. His father had found work abroad as a central heating engineer, and it paid so much more than what they could earn at home in Yugoslavia, that they determined it was worth whatever emotional loss might be suffered by their two sons to leave, returning once they'd earned enough to build a house and give their children a better life. It must have been an aching decision but, at the time, it was the sort of decision that many people in their situation would have made. But that did not make it any easier for little Janez and his brother, who spent these three formative years in the arms of their loving grandmother, Pavla.

When his parents finally did return and were calling out to Janez, the mixed emotions of his age and their absence led him to initially hide from them. When he didn't respond to their calls, his father was concerned that he had fallen into the stream and charged forward, in his Sunday best, ruining his clothes, expensively bought abroad, and plowed through the water in search of his son to save him.

This is JB's earliest memory, and it is a powerful one. His first memories related to food are at the home of his grandmother. Pavla was particularly poor and they lived in a modest house, poor enough that it was a treat to get a meal of meat or eggs. He fondly remembers her cooking eggs fried in pork cracklings. And it is fitting, then, that one of his most famous dishes at his eponymous restaurant, JB in Ljubljana—ranked among the 100 best restaurants in the world in 2010 and in 2012 listed among the 10 best in Europe—is a throwback, a Proustian sense memory experience recalling those fried eggs in cracklings, but refined to the level of a high-end restaurant of the sort he has run now for two decades. JB serves a fresh egg yolk onto which sparking-hot oil from cracklings is poured directly at the table. The heat of the oil ideally cooks the egg, and there is house-made bread for dipping. It couldn't be simpler. It is heavenly. It is heartfelt. It is integral to his story.

━━━━━━

The JB restaurant is located on the ground floor of the Triglav Insurance Building, which was designed by modernist architect, Jože Plečnik, the greatest ever Slovenian-born architect. Established in 1992, JB the restaurant was the first fine-dining establishment in newly-independent Slovenia. That made JB, the chef, the first to bring nouvelle cuisine to Yugoslavia, and of course to his homeland, the Republic of Slovenia, which declared independence in 1991. Prior to JB's return to Slovenia, after many years working at high-end restaurants in Austria, Slovenians had rarely heard of, and still less frequently encountered, things like carpaccio, ceviche, foams and gels, or even meat cooked rare, rather than well done. He was a revolutionary, and so remains.

JB was introduced to exotic foods early on. His father was a bon vivant and frequently returned to Germany for work, always bringing back something unusual to eat, at least by Yugoslav standards. White asparagus and blue cheese were all but unheard of. So, when his father brought these delicacies back from abroad, it was the talk of the town. During one of these parental sojourns abroad, when JB and his brother were with their grandmother, the area around which they lived was flooded, and they had to leave their home for a period of time. They were taken in by some neighbors who were a bit better off, occupying a two-story house and stocked with foods that were beyond the budget of JB's family. The one he remembers most fondly was oatmeal. He had never encountered oatmeal before, but ate it for breakfast while staying with this kind neighbor family. These sort of sense memories are among the most powerful: what a beloved family member cooked for us when we were little strikes a bell that may have receded in our minds, but which still resounds clearly when struck.

It is particularly striking for audiences from the Western world, for whom just about everything one could wish for has regularly been available whenever one might like, to look back at a time when a country like Yugoslavia had a quite limited palate, not due to tastes, but to availability. Slovenia was always the most independent of the former Yugoslav nations, with open borders and the ability to go on shopping trips to Austria and Italy. But what was available in Yugoslavia was restricted largely to what was produced in Yugoslavia or by ally nations. So, things like coffee and bananas and chocolate were exotic commodities, and everything which was purchased abroad was given a higher status and was considered more desirable, just as people who studied abroad or had successes abroad were assigned a higher social status. So, while it may be difficult for us to imagine parents deciding to leave their two young sons for several years, some sympathy for this mindset also helps to explain why JB himself would later go abroad for work, even when he had young children at home.

JB remembers being asked by his grandmother what job he might like to have, as choosing a high school meant choosing a vocational school, at that time. First, he wanted to be a construction worker, but Pavla's husband had that occupation and she was aware that he was outdoors in all sorts of weather, in rain and snow, and she suggested instead that young JB become a cook. She explained that this would mean that he would always have something to eat and something to drink and be inside and dry and warm. Such were the priorities for a poor Yugoslav family at the time. So, he chose a cooking school in Ljubljana, though he was mocked by his classmates because, in those days, cooking was more of a female profession and also something that was considered the métier of only those who couldn't do anything else. Times have changed and now cooks can very quickly become celebrities, but this was several decades ago.

JB's first job was as a cook at the Tourist Hotel in Ljubljana, which is on the site of the current City Hotel. He also worked for the cafeteria of Energetika, the capital city's main power company. There he was dishing out cafeteria staples, which meant things like cutlets with mashed potatoes, goulash, pasta, sausages and sauerkraut, Wiener schnitzel, salads of lettuce, strudel . . . For anglophone readers, this may all sound somewhat exotic, but these are the everyday classics in Slovenia, a country that has many of its own particular specialties, but which is heavily influenced by the four nations that border it: Austria, Italy, Croatia, and Hungary. In the north of Slovenia, Austrian influence is most heavily felt, and that is the region from which JB hails. This means cream sauces, cooking with butter and wine and pork cracklings, sausages and sauerkraut, and schnitzel and strudel. In the Western region, there is a heavy Italian influence, with olive oil and fish, truffles, pasta, and risotto. Throughout Slovenia, you have the popular influence of foods from the other Yugoslav republics, particularly Bosnian and Serbian grilled meats and baked savory pies and fluffy flat breads. And in the east, adjacent to Hungary, there are dishes with smoked paprika under the influences that blow off the Pannonian plain. This makes Slovenia truly a crossroads for different food types, with the addition of its own autonomous inventions, for example gibanica and potica cakes.

Cooking at the cafeteria was a great gig for young JB, as he was in the kitchen in Ljubljana during the winter, but during the summer, he was assigned to the company's summer holiday camp, where staff members could go for a free week-long beach vacation every summer, on the Croatian island of Rab. He would make simple food there and be done very quickly, so he could spend a lot of the time for which he was getting paid on other activities, especially on the gorgeous beaches and in the crystal blue waters of the Adriatic. It also meant that he had so many hours on paper racked up in the summer that when he got back to the capital in the wintertime, he didn't have to work quite as much.

It was at this time that JB made the decision to go abroad to expand his horizons, but also to earn some money. He had recently gotten married to his wife, Ema, and their first child was born, their daughter Nina. It must have been a tough decision, but he was schooled by his father's experience and decided it was worthwhile to go just across the border into Austria to gain experience, but mostly to earn money in order to support his family and buy a house and make a better life for them. He came to this decision by leaving matters in the hands of fate. He read of a call for chefs at a famous Austrian restaurant on the Faaker See, a lake not far across the border, called Der Tschebull. He hand-wrote a letter applying for a position and mailed it off, not thinking much of it. His colleagues mocked his laid-back approach, thinking that the young JB would not even get a reply. He had almost forgotten about it when, one day, an American stretch limousine pulled up in front of his home. Inside were the owners of Der Tschebull. They said they'd like to hire him. But when he asked how much the job paid, they offered a salary not much higher than what he was already earning–not enough to warrant leaving his family. So, he politely declined. A few weeks later, the limo was back, and they substantially raised the offer. He was in.

He moved to Austria and eagerly dug into a cooking approach that was far more refined than what he was used to at home. Der Tschebull was committed to nouvelle cuisine, a movement largely unknown in Yugoslavia. In Austria, he studied as best he could, learning not only cooking techniques but also reading food magazines in German, of the sort that he could never get his hands on in Yugoslavia, and really developing from a cook into a proper chef. The restaurant was hugely popular and sophisticated, but also a major operation, employing some ten chefs in the offseason and twenty during the high season. He honed techniques but also expanded his horizons; for instance, learning to serve game meat rare, something anathema back home. He spent some time in the winter cooking elsewhere, in Tirol, but was a major force in the kitchen of Der Tschebull. When he began to toy with the idea of opening his own restaurant back in Slovenia, they were keen to keep him. They offered a substantial hike in salary, but he decided that it was time to take a gamble. At thirty years old, he felt he had much to show the folks back at home.

It was a risk, but one he felt he was ready to take. He scraped together some capital, borrowed and maneuvered, and rented space in Domžale, a town close to his native Trzin and some ten minutes from Ljubljana. This was the first incarnation of JB. He would be in the kitchen, his wife Ema helping front of house and keeping the books.

From the start, JB decided that his restaurant would offer something new and different, the sort of food that he had learned to prepare, which was avant-garde in Slovenia in 1992, just a year after it gained independence from Yugoslavia. He would prepare everything in-house. Vegetables would be fresh. Meat would be cooked medium rare. He would offer fish carpaccio and handmade noodles. Each dish would have its own sauce. None of this sounds particularly revolutionary today, but at the time and place, it was mind-blowing. His prices were relatively high, and he didn't know how to promote his quality. Early days were slow. He would prepare meals for thirty and throw away most of it. It was disheartening, but he stuck to his guns. Every day he prepared fresh food, putting his all into it. Something had to give.

His big break came when he received a surprise call from the office of the Slovenian prime minister. Janez Drnovšek would like to come to lunch. Would that be okay? You bet it would. JB thought it was a practical joke, until the prime minister arrived. He became a regular, and word slowly spread. Guests came to JB because they'd heard he offered something different. He was cooking in a way no one else in Yugoslavia was, nor would they for many years to come.

The next stride forward came when the director of the national insurance company, Triglav Insurance, invited him to move his restaurant from Domžale to the heart of the capital, on the ground floor of the Triglav headquarters, just across from the main train station. JB liked the idea, but when he asked what the rent would be, he was quoted a price so outrageously high that the monthly rent roughly matched his restaurant's entire income over a three-month period. So, he politely declined. But politely declining had, more than once, proved a good move for JB. About a year later, the director came back and made a better offer. She had tried out several chefs in the place in question, and none had been a hit. She'd love to have him, she said. JB again inquired how much the rent would be. However much you want it to be, she said. That sounded like a good deal. He named a reasonable price, and she accepted. It was on.

In his elegant new location, JB and his restaurant blossomed. They had regular business, and good reviews, but it was still a small-scale operation. At one point one of JB's staff chefs left suddenly to start his own restaurant and took six assistants from JB's kitchen with him. In one month, JB essentially lost his team. But he is the sort of person who is determined to show himself and others that nothing will stand in his way. He redoubled his own efforts, less reliant on assistants, and this proved to be a challenge that pushed him from excellence to brilliance. His children, raised in the unusual rhythm of a restaurateur's life (home only in the mornings and on Sundays, at work until late in the evening), followed their father's footsteps. His daughter Nina worked as a sommelier at JB before becoming a chef at her own restaurant in another part of the country, and recently returned to JB. His son, Tomaž, recently completed a stage at a Michelin-starred restaurant Arzak in San Sebastián, Spain, and joined the JB kitchen. The whole family now works in the restaurant.

From 2000–2008, JB restaurant was regularly fully-booked, with waiting lists. It was just before the other chefs of Slovenia caught onto the trend he had begun. Today, Slovenia is acknowledged as a significant world food destination with numerous acclaimed chefs. But they describe JB as the godfather of modern cooking in this region, and he had a decade's head start. He never sought notoriety. He turned down numerous chances to open restaurants abroad, to franchise, to become a TV chef, to advertise for major corporations. On Sundays, when the restaurant is closed, JB enjoys an hour or two of lounging around the house, before he gets antsy, eager for Monday to come around so he can get back to work. Being a cook is a lifestyle, he admits, and you have to embrace it as such.

He travels as an invited guest at major festivals, he rubs elbows with everyone from Ferran Adrià to Rene Redzepi, from Nobu Matsuhisa (who wrote the Foreword for this book) to Heinz Beck to Massimo Bottura. But his home has always been his restaurant's kitchen. He doesn't like to leave his cooking to others, feeling best when he is in his whites, dancing from station to station. He employs assistants but supervises everything. He also regularly takes in young cooks, some with little training, if he sees that they work hard and show promise. He is patient and generous. He does not yell or grandstand. He even takes phone reservations himself (if your call to the restaurant rings more than five times without someone picking up, it will be JB who greets you to take your reservation).

Passionate, hard work paid off. The critics came. They loved what they ate. JB's efforts were focused inward—it has always been about the food, about the time spent in the kitchen. So many younger chefs go directly for celebrity, to become a brand before they've put in the years of hard work to earn that status. JB is the opposite. He has let celebrity come to him, but even now, having been praised by just about every media outlet that matters, he will still be there to cook for you (and even take your call) when you go to his eponymous restaurant.

This book explores JB's homeland, Slovenia, by crisscrossing the country to visit his preferred producers of what he considers to be the finest ingredients he can find. He selected twenty ingredients, which involved visiting twenty remote locations, from the shores of the Adriatic to the Alps, from the Pannonian plain to turquoise rivers and rolling hills. I was lucky enough to tag along. The resulting book presents Slovenia through its raw ingredients. While JB is the through-line, the protagonist, each chapter presents the ingredient and the farmers and producers of those ingredients, who are the heroes on this quest to find the best of Slovenia through the travels of its superlative chef. I was delighted to be one of the sidekicks on this adventure, tasked with writing the profiles of the producers and the ingredients and "forced" to eat all manner of delights with JB, a man who I am proud to call a friend now, after so many days and winding road trips together that helped me to explore my adopted country. We traveled with Matjaž Tančič, a young Slovenian photographer who lives in China and is among the best in the world, the winner of numerous awards, including the 2013 Sony World Photographer of the Year, with his assistant, Tjaša, and with the brilliant food photographer, Manca Jevšček. It was a dream team and the best way I can imagine to get to know Slovenia better. We are delighted to present to you what is more than a cookbook. It is also a travelogue, a portrait of a wondrous, quirky country, and a love story about passion for cooking, for eating, for the best ingredients that this wonderland has to offer. Welcome to Slovenia . . . and *dober tek.*

A FOOD ROAD TRIP
ACROSS SLOVENIA

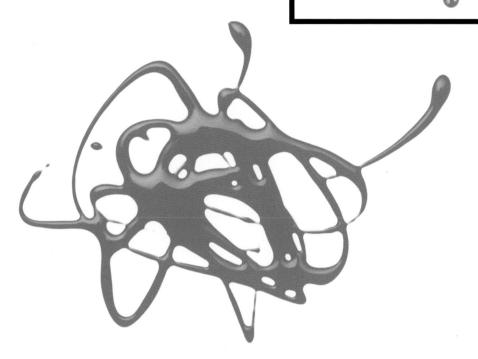

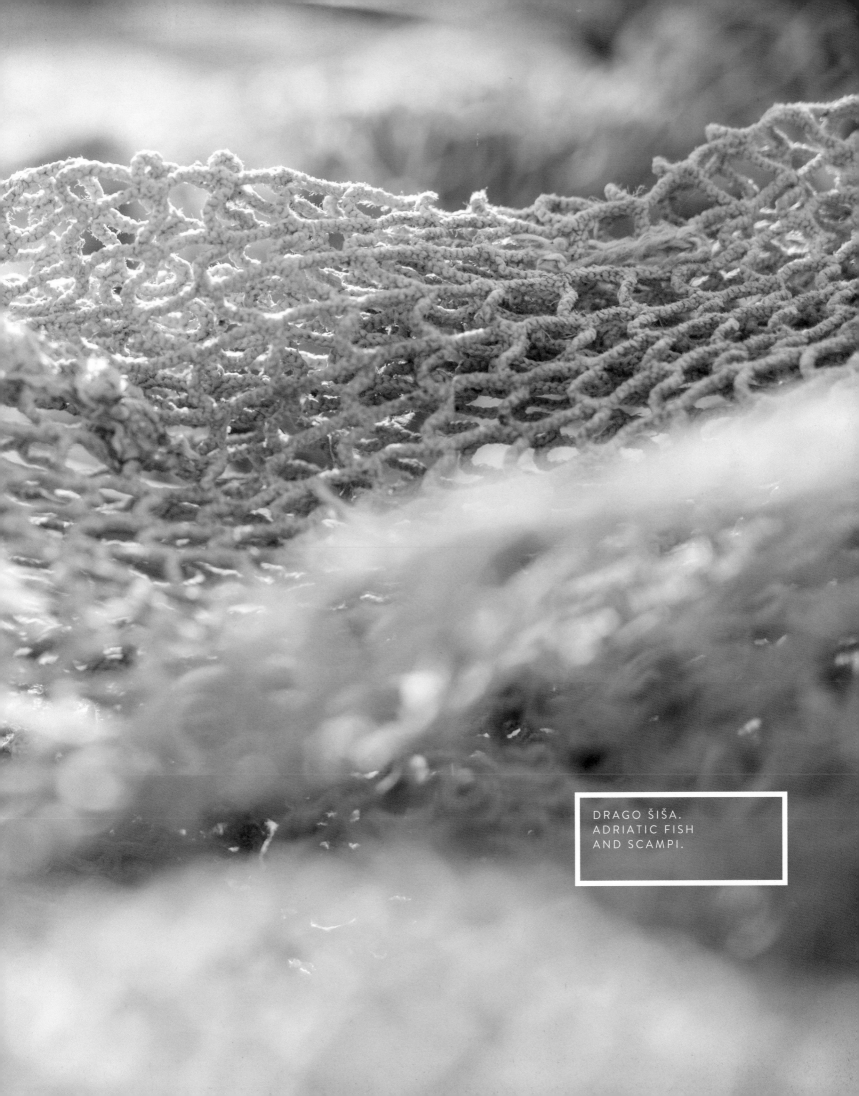

DRAGO ŠIŠA.
ADRIATIC FISH
AND SCAMPI.

ADRIATIC FISH AND SCAMPI

The first thing you need to know about the story of JB's fisherman is that our stalwart photographer, while snapping photos on the calm seas off the Istrian peninsula, managed to trip and fall into the ocean, very expensive camera and all. This was the most dramatic moment in an otherwise smooth voyage, but the smoothness was not self-evident when the ship first set out.

In the interest of full disclosure, I will say that I was not on the voyage. I am not a very good sailor and the idea of spending twelve hours on the sea, in a small and potentially bumpy boat, was not my idea of a party. This fear of sea sickness was compounded when word came in that there was a *burja* (bora) wind approaching, weather so inclement that the fishing trip, while not canceled, was warned against for us, for fear that it would be too tempest-tossed for our comfort and safety. With this news, I happily excused myself and it looked as if JB and our photographer, Matjaž, and his assistant, Tjaša, would be unable to set out. I left them to head back home from the tiny village of Krnički Porat, on the coast of Istria, about two and a half hours from my home in Kamnik. I was on the road when I got a message that, at the last moment, our team had said, "Screw it, let's go anyway," and hopped aboard the fishing boat just as they were pulling out.

It turned out that the fears about that otherwise wonderful wind, the *burja* that blows across the limestone *karst* plateaus of coastal Slovenia and Istria, drying the hanging hocks of ham just enough to transform them into heavenly prosciutto, were wilder than the reality. When I got the report back the next day, it turned out that it had been quite calm, a sea that would not have even troubled my ropey stomach. But Matjaž had managed to fall in, all the same.

JB gets his fish from a single boat led by a humble captain, Drago Šiša, and his son Daniel, and their three-man crew. They catch fish and shellfish using dragnets in a system that has been in place for millennia, and which is both simple and ingenious. When they set off in a small boat, they wait until they are at least a mile off the coast and into the Kvarner, the sea between Pula, Rijeka, and the island of Krk. At that point they drop expansive nets that are designed with gaps in the netting small enough to catch fish of a minimum size or larger, but large enough to let fish that would be too small to keep anyway swim through. They drop the nets behind the boat and then continue chugging out in a straight line for approximately six hours. At that point, they turn around and head back in towards port, dragging the nets behind them. When they are about two hours away from port, they pull in the nets and sort and clean their haul. By the time they have arrived back at port, the nets are in and the fish have been cleaned, with parts that nobody wants discarded into the ocean to feed other sea creatures, who are less particular than we humans. The load arrives back at port on ice, seated in Styrofoam trays and already sorted by quality and type and arranged by weight. It's a very good use of time and nicely efficient. It also means that the majority of the work is done during just half of the ride home, with a fairly low-key voyage out for all but the last few hours. This gave Matjaž plenty of time to take photos and fall into the ocean.

By the time the boat returns to shore, they will have radioed ahead with details about their catch. JB will receive a call or a text about what is available, will place an order, and the fish will be driven up to him once or twice a week, as necessary. It doesn't get any fresher for a restaurant at the foot of the Alps—fish just two or three hours out of the ocean. Then other orders go to top restaurants elsewhere, most of them in Italy, while a portion also goes to market.

JB likes to get sea bream (*orada*) and sea bass (*brancin*), as these are the culinary stars of the Adriatic Sea, and are considerably better when caught wild than when purchased from a fish farm (although there is one fish farm, as we will see, that produces sea bass that is as close as any in the world to approaching the quality of those caught in the wild). If there are occasional oddities that come up in the nets, like the relatively rare, larger-sized lobsters that sometimes appear, JB will get a special phone call. He will often have a client who he knows so well that he is aware that they are fans of a certain specialty and will come to the restaurant when they hear that JB has the ingredients to make it. Landing special types of fish or a very expensive lobster will often allow JB to in turn land one of his favorite customers at the restaurant, as well, coming in specially for a unique plate made by an acknowledged master, just for them.

Most of the captain's cargo is, apart from fish, in the form of cuttlefish, octopus, shellfish, and scampi, which are available year-round. JB says that the Kvarner waters produce the best scampi he's tasted, the world over. They'll haul in an average of eleven pounds (five kilos) of scampi in one night, part of a total of around 220 pounds (one-hundred kilos) of fish per trip. The flotsam and jetsam of the haul results in goods that might not be quite exciting enough to feature as an entree themselves, but which are packed with flavor, and are used to make a traditional Istrian dish that the fishermen particularly enjoy and remember versions of cooked up by grandmothers: *brodet*. It is a sensual, richly-filled fish soup to which just about anything caught and left over after market sales can be added, to flavor the broth, which is eaten with a spoon or sipped from a bowl or sopped up with crusty bread. This is the dish that all of the fishermen on board, each asked independently, said that they most enjoy and dream about when they're out at sea, particularly when it's a cold or wet night.

And what about the photographer in the ocean, you're wondering? JB was napping on the deck at the time and remembers only hearing one of the crew members shouting that there was a man overboard. Matjaž was unharmed and quickly swam back to the boat. The camera was not so lucky. Unfortunately, it was also uninsured. That very fancy bit of equipment was lugged back on board, to see if there was any chance it could be dried out and salvaged. Salvaged it was, but it was no longer functional. Instead, Matjaž turned it into a particularly expensive and unique desk lamp, which graces his apartment back home in Shanghai.

OCTOPUS COOKED IN ITS OWN JUICES, WITH TOMATO, AVOCADO, AND CUTTLEFISH CHIPS

Place the octopus into the sink and grate the fresh turnip over it, then knead them together to clean the octopus, and rinse with clean water. When the octopus is clean, carefully bash it with an empty glass bottle. This will soften the tentacles so that they remain tender after cooking.

Combine the water, kombu, soy sauce, halved or roughly chopped onion and tomato, rosemary, and salt in a saucepan. Bring to a boil, cook for a few minutes, and leave to cool.

Place the octopus into a vacuum sealer bag suitable for sous vide cooking, pour in the kombu and soy soup, and carefully seal it. Cook the octopus for 2 hours and 10 minutes in a combi-steamer, using the steam function. Afterwards place the bag into ice water until it cools completely. Remove the octopus from the bag and cut it into small pieces, reserving 1¼ cups (300 ml) of the soup for the sauce.

3¼ pounds (1.5 kg) octopus
1 turnip
4¼ cups (1 L) water
1 sheet kombu kelp
½ cup (100 ml) soy sauce
1 onion, halved or roughly chopped
1 tomato, halved or roughly chopped
1 sprig rosemary
Salt

SAUCE:
Strain 1¼ cups (300 ml) of the liquid in which the octopus was cooked, pour it into a tall container, and blend with an immersion blender, slowly adding both oils to obtain a mayonnaise.

1¼ cups (300 ml) liquid, reserved from cooking the octopus
½ cup (100 ml) olive oil
½ cup (100 ml) canola oil

SAMPHIRE:
In a saucepan combine the water, vinegar, and salt. Bring to a boil, then add the washed samphire leaves and leave to cool. Leave the samphire in the liquid for as long as possible to develop the flavor.

2¼ cups (500 ml) water
½ cup (100 ml) white vinegar
Salt
7 ounces (200 g) rock samphire

CUTTLEFISH CHIPS:
Boil the tapioca pearls in salted water for 20 minutes. When they are cooked, drain them and put into a small saucepan, add the cuttlefish ink, and cook for 6 minutes. Spread the paste onto a silicone mat and dry for 4 hours in a convection oven at 140°F (60°C). When the tapioca is dry, break it into large pieces and fry for a few seconds in oil heated to 325°F (165°C), to obtain chips. (It is easiest to dip the pieces in the oil using tongs.)

1¾ ounces (50 g) tapioca pearls
1 teaspoon cuttlefish ink
Oil for frying
Salt

AVOCADO:
Peel the avocado, remove the pit, and pass the flesh through a fine sieve. Season with salt and lemon juice and whisk to get a smooth purée.

1 avocado
Salt
Juice of ½ lemon

TOMATO:
Briefly blanch the tomatoes and peel them. Combine the wine, vinegar, and sugar in a saucepan and bring to a boil. Roughly chop the tomatoes, add them to the liquid, cook for 5 minutes, and set aside to cool.

12 cherry tomatoes
½ cup (100 ml) white wine
¼ cup (50 ml) white balsamic vinegar
2 tablespoons (30 g) sugar

TO SERVE:
Place the sauce on a plate first, followed by the octopus, avocado purée, tomato sauce, and the marinated samphire. Finally, drizzle with olive oil, decorate with nasturtium leaves and cuttlefish chips, and serve.

Olive oil
Nasturtium leaves

KVARNER SCAMPI WITH TAPIOCA, CAVIAR, AND LEMONGRASS FOAM

Chop the lemongrass and cook it in the salted milk for 8 minutes. Leave in the fridge overnight to infuse.

3 stalks lemongrass
1 cup (200 ml) full fat milk
¼ teaspoon (1.5 g) salt

Peel the shrimp and de-vein them with tweezers.

8 jumbo shrimp (1 pound or 450 g)
1 tablespoon clarified butter (ghee)
Fleur de sel

Roughly chop the onion. Heat the olive oil in a saucepan, add the onion and the heads and claws of the shrimp. Fry for 15 minutes, then cover with water, add the lemon, sliced ginger, and salt and simmer on low heat for 1 hour. Drain, add the cream, and cook a further half-hour to make a nice sauce.

1 onion
¼ cup (50 ml) olive oil
Jumbo shrimp heads and claws (10 ounces or 280 g)
3 cups (700 ml) water
¼ lemon
1 tablespoon (10 g) ginger root
½ teaspoon (2.5 g) salt
1 cup (200 ml) whipping cream

Pour the tapioca into the 6⅓ cups (1.5 L) boiling water and stir for at least half a minute to ensure that it does not stick to the bottom of the pan. Cook for 20 minutes, stirring occasionally, then remove from heat and set aside for 5 minutes. Drain the tapioca and rinse it with cold water.

½ cup (100 g) tapioca pearls
6⅓ cups (1.5 L) water
1 teaspoon (5 g) salt

Place the tapioca in the cream sauce and heat through. Quickly fry the shrimp in ghee so they are still raw in the center, and season with salt.

Heat the lemongrass milk, strain it, and blend with an immersion blender to make foam.

TO SERVE:
Spoon the tapioca into a deep bowl and arrange two halved shrimp tails on top. Add a tiny bit of caviar and some lemongrass foam. Drizzle with olive oil.

1 teaspoon Iranian caviar
Olive oil

IRENA FONDA,
FONDA FISH FARM.
SEA BASS.

SEA BASS

Farm-raised fish just does not taste as good as wild. That is the rule that the world seems to agree on. But there is one family challenging it, and they have come closest of anyone around the globe to equaling the taste of line-caught sea bass, but with fish raised on an aquatic farm.

This time, the photographer was in the water on purpose. Matjaž is a specialist photographer in a number of categories. Along with being generally considered among the world's most respected and renowned young photographers, he was the Sony World Photographer of the Year in the category of 3D photographs, and he also specializes in underwater photography. So, he was well-suited to snap away at the thousands of sea bass in cyclone-shaped submarine netted pens that hang adrift in the Adriatic Sea, just off the shore of Piran and a stone's throw from the salt pans we would later visit.

How can farm-raised fish approach or match the quality of those living in the wild? That was the puzzle and challenge that the Fonda family laid out for themselves. Irena Fonda spoke to me over a glass of local wine on the shore beside her office, which is modern and sleek, but which sits adjacent to a sort of sea barn decorated in all manner of Yugoslav memorabilia, alongside antique boating supplies and a gaping shark's jaw lined with teeth. Her family set up Fonda Fish Farm, a farm for *brancin*, sea bass, with the goal of being the first in the world to produce sea bass on a farm that was indistinguishable on the plate from the wild ones.

It was a challenge fitting for her family, as all members of it are biologists. Her father originally wanted to build an underwater park with a reef, set up to encourage snorkeling and scuba diving off the Piran coast. But meeting with no luck on the bureaucratic front, he instead shifted to aquatic agriculture as a pet project. They would raise only sea bass, a fish that is considered the cream of the Adriatic—the tastiest and most sought-after of the sea's offerings. It would be the northernmost fish farm in the Mediterranean and would be special indeed.

Irena's family hand-picks all the young female sea bass that they incorporate into their farm. This is already an unusual step. Irena studies them and her brother Lean has a team of scuba divers working full-time for him, to make sure that they are growing right. They take their time raising the fish, too. Whereas most farms rush to sell and see profit, Fonda sea bass grow for four to five years before they are sold. This is a very lengthy process, along the lines of a vineyard producing fine wine or a distillery aging whiskey, requiring patience before you see any profit. Fonda will pay more for the babies than anyone else, and at first she was mocked by competitors for paying a cent or so more per baby fish.

One of the problems that the Fondas have run into is that their buyers also seem to have no eye out for quality. They say they can buy sea bass more cheaply from other, more distant fish farms, and their customers don't seem to appreciate the difference. Theirs may taste better, but their clientele do not notice, and want to pay as little as possible for lunch. Such an approach is understandable from a fiscal standpoint, if a diner is watching his pennies, but provokes a sigh from those who see it as a sign of the times, that quantity and savings are more important than quality of experience. But there is an audience for the finer things in life, even if it may not be among the Slovenian locals. From the start, 96 percent of Fonda's production has been bought by high-end Italian restaurants and fish markets. There, they seem very happy to pay a bit more for better quality.

Irena appreciates JB immensely, for his attention to detail with his ingredients. He rolls up his sleeves and doesn't bother with the price tag. He tests out the product, cooking it in a variety of ways, tasting it, and sharing it with friends and colleagues, before making an objective decision, based on empirical research. For instance, she says, he noticed that, in winter, the Fonda sea bass required more fat in the pan to cook properly, meaning that he had to add more oil or butter. He was the only chef to notice this, and Irena praises him for the observation that, in fact, in wintertime sea bass lose some of their fat content, as they expend more energy to stay warm, and so the meat bought in winter does require the introduction of more fat to the cooking process. She shakes her head in admiration.

But the fish are not only well-prepared after "harvesting." They have a pretty sweet life before they hit the kitchen. They are tended to by a team of scuba-diving farmers and are hand-fed twice a day. To illustrate how the farming process works, Irena shows me blown-up underwater photographs of the fish, in a huge spiraling silver glinting whirlwind, and closeups of individuals. She points out that, in hundreds of specimens, there is not a single one with a visible deformity, like an overbite. They are all completely identical and that, she says, means the highest level of quality and consistency.

The Fonda team keeps a close watch on the mental state of the fish, too. Fish can be stressed, which may sound like a joke, but can affect the quality of their meat. When they first came to her farm, in a large cistern truck, she noticed them clustering at the far corner of the cistern, trying to avoid being poured into the tanks that would eventually take them into their floating net-pens in the ocean, which contain them but give them plenty of room to swim. By the following day, they will have adapted, swimming happily, a sign that they like their new environment. The Fonda fish pens have many fewer fish per enclosure than most farms do, to give them the most space to move and develop and stretch their muscles, for the muscles are the meat.

It all results in a far better product. If JB serves up Fonda sea bass alongside wild line-caught sea bass, and offers the exact same preparation, blind, to different chefs, he guesses that 90 percent of them would not recognize the difference. With the general public, an even smaller percentage would distinguish between the two, such is the level of quality. When it comes to farming fish, the knowledge and science and passion and attention to detail are poured in and come out on the plates of the best chefs, like JB, for whom taste is all the difference.

Next up, the Fonda family plans to try raising *orada*, gilthead bream. One can only wait and wonder.

MARINATED SEA BASS WITH CORIANDER, LIME, FRESH CUCUMBER JUICE, AND MARINATED RADISHES

Fillet the fish and remove all bones.

Thinly peel the lime. Cook the zest in boiling water, blanching it for 15 seconds. Repeat 3 more times, changing water each time. This softens the flavor, so that it will marry well with the fish.

Squeeze the juice from the lime, combine with kombucha, and season with salt. Cut the fish into ¾-inch pieces and cover with the marinade. Marinate for 2 hours.

1 sea bass (approx. 1½ pounds or 700 g)
1 lime
½ cup (100 ml) kombucha
Fleur de sel and salt

RADISHES:
Thinly slice the radishes. Boil the water with vinegar and sugar, then add the radishes. Transfer into a plastic container and vacuum three times in a vacuum machine (without a bag). Leave to marinate for half an hour.

5 radishes
1¼ cups (300 ml) water
¼ cup (50 ml) white vinegar
3 tablespoons (40 g) sugar

CUCUMBERS:
Roughly chop the cucumbers and juice them using a juicer. Season the juice with salt.

10½ ounces (300 g) cucumbers

TO SERVE:
Remove the fish from the marinade and arrange on a plate. Add cucumber juice, radishes, pieces of cooked lime zest, and a pinch of fleur de sel. You may add a slice or two of fresh cucumber, too, if desired.

BLACK RISOTTO WITH CUTTLEFISH, SEA BASS, AND SMALL SCALLOPS

———————

Clean the fish and scallops, season with salt, and cover with olive oil. Leave to marinate for half an hour.

⅓ pound (150 g) fillet sea bass
24 small scallops (meat only)
¾ cup (150 ml) olive oil

Clean the cuttlefish (see below), taking care with the ink sacs. Remove the membranes and cut the flesh into small pieces. Squeeze the ink (you will get about 1½ tablespoons or 20 g) out of the sacs and combine with olive oil in a small saucepan.

⅔ pound (300 g) fresh cuttlefish
¼ cup (50 ml) olive oil

Chop the shallots and fry them in olive oil until soft, then add the cuttlefish pieces and fry for 3 more minutes. Add the rice and stir well to coat the grains. Add some fish stock, which must be hot. Stir constantly, gradually adding stock to the risotto, and cook for 10 minutes. Then add the oil with ink and continue cooking. When the rice absorbs all the liquid, add more hot stock. Stir constantly for another 8 minutes. The rice should be al dente.

½ cup (100 g) shallots
2 tablespoons (30 ml) olive oil
8½ ounces (240 g) carnaroli rice
4¼ cups (1 L) hot fish stock
3½ tablespoons (50 g) frozen butter
Salt

Remove from the heat, add the frozen butter, and stir until the risotto is creamy.

TO SERVE:
Place the hot risotto in a bowl, arranging the fish and scallops on top.

TO CLEAN CUTTLEFISH:
First remove the bone and pull the meat apart at the same spot. From the inside, remove the head and innards. The ink sac can be recognized by its metallic blue color. Remove it carefully. Pull the membranes away from the flesh.

DARIO GLAVINA,
THE PIRAN SALT PANS.
FLEUR DE SEL.

FLEUR DE SEL

The salt pans sit on the sea beside the town of Piran, an endlessly lovely scramble of terracotta-colored houses and miniature palazzi, spiked with two dramatic church bell towers, hugging the Slovenian coast, and a stone's throw from the Fonda Fish Farm. If it recalls a teacup-sized Venice, that is no coincidence–this was an outpost of the Venetian Republic for centuries. It has likewise been a center for the gathering of sea salt since the time of the Roman Empire, when salt was so valuable, as a flavor enhancer and preserver of meat, that it was sometimes used as currency (hence the word "salary," which derives from *salaria*, Latin for "wages," which itself derives from *sal*, or "salt").

The principle of the salt pans is not simple. Before the harvesting season, a *petola* is carefully restored and prepared. Each *petola* is a cultivated layer of cyanobacteria, algae, gypsum, and minerals, which divides salt from mud and enables the production of pure white salt. This technique was introduced in the fourteenth century and the tradition has been kept alive. In a complicated system with basins, mounds, channels, wooden barriers, free falls, siphons, and pumps, the seawater evaporates, aided by sun and wind, until it arrives at the appropriate density, and finally reaches the salt pans, where workers pour it into their crystallization basins. Here it continues to evaporate, and on the bottom of the basins salt crystals appear. Salt can then be pushed into piles, with large wooden toothless rakes (called a *gavero*), shoveled into wheelbarrows (*karele*), and transported on rails from the basins to the concrete platform (*pjacal*) to dry further in the sun.

But first they collect a thin crust, which appears in the surface of the salt water in basins. This is fleur de sel or flower of salt. (The salt destined for other, less refined purposes, such as fine-grinding, is harvested from layers below.) In this rawest form, fleur de sel, salt is at its best. It's the crème de la crème of condiments, with nothing in it but itself–no anticoagulants, not the product of extensive handling and exposure, as salt sometimes is when mined. This is just sea water minus the water, raked into place by a charming man in a surprisingly hipster-friendly striped bathing suit and an oversized sun hat that recalls the headgear of rice farmers.

It wasn't easy to find Dario Glavina. We first met the charming Martina, a young woman who had only recently begun to work at the salt flats, catering to the surprisingly high number of tourists who come to admire them. We were looking for a farmer to interview and photograph, and appeared to be out of luck, as there was no one to be seen across the expanse of flats that drifted seaward, towards the glancing sun. The harvesting season was nearing its end, and salt farmers are usually at work in the morning, then they go home for lunch and to rest, and then come back late in the afternoon, when the heat subsides. Then Martina volunteered that she had a family friend who might be perfect, if she could reach him by phone.

Dario was indeed available but couldn't arrive for a few hours. We quickly adopted Martina and insisted on buying her lunch as a thank-you, while we waited. We adjourned to a famous fish restaurant, where we were (very slowly) served a surfboard-sized plate of shellfish. Only after we'd paid the bill did our waiter realize that he had been catering to the famous JB.

Salt farmers are in short supply, and the entire, elaborate bevy of salt pans is under-staffed. As Dario explained, this sort of work is physically difficult, under-paid, and requires passion and enthusiasm to be any good at it. The result is that there are very few salt farmers remaining, and most of the staff are shipped-in laborers who perhaps lack the attention to detail and admiration for tradition that Dario wears proudly. If any youngsters are looking for a good farming work/study program, this is about as good as it gets.

Dario smiles incessantly, never giving away, through gritted teeth or expression of fatigue, just how labor-intensive this work is. The format has not changed in centuries. Each farmer is assigned their salt field, called salt "fund" or *štabile*, and made of four rows of six identically-sized salt pans, called *cavedini*. A stretch of railroad track runs between two rows of pans, and a small gurney, loaded with half a ton of salt, rides along it. As the sun evaporates the water, crystals of coarse sea salt are left behind on the bottom of the basins, collected into piles, while on the surface, the precious fleur de sel appears, looking like over-sized snowflakes that, surreally, proliferate under the hot sun. Farmers like Dario move from one of their pans to another, using a rake to push the salt flakes into piles. They load these piles onto the gurney, roll it along the track back to the stretch of solid earth behind their salt pans, and dump it into an enormous pile. There it remains, under the sun, for as long as it takes to get as dry as possible. It is then shoveled onto trucks and brought to the Piran Salt factory for packaging. Nothing else goes into it. It's just saltwater, sun, and Dario.

JB admits to using Piran fleur de sel to finish many of his dishes, and he cruises through many containers a week. His only objection is that they are packaged for home use, in 9-ounce (250 g) bins, and he wishes he could buy a kilo box at a time.

Dario pulls back a tarp to reveal a small mountain of salt flakes, which we immediately mentally convert into cash. That must be hundreds of euros worth of salt, if not thousands, which makes the extremely modest salary of the salt farmers worth their salt—or obliges us to take them with a grain of salt (I'm torn between stretched analogies).

We're encouraged to scoop up some of the not-quite-dry fleur de sel and taste it. Now, I normally think of salt as enhancing flavors, and I know what a salty taste is (usually brought to mind when something is over-salted). But this tastes delicious as is, not too salty (despite the fact that it is, literally, just salt). My only analogy is to water. There's water that tastes good and water that doesn't really register with us and water that tastes bad, even though it's all, theoretically, H_2O. This is like no salt I've tried.

Part of the appeal is that it is not finely-ground, nor is it in the form of the coarse ground salt that so nicely studs charred steaks. Each flake of salt, like a flake of snow, is unique and an odd shape. That means lots of surface area, and a slower dissolution on the tongue, as well as a texture that gives a pleasant almost-crunch entirely lacking from even the excellent finely-ground salt from shakers made of this exact same product but harvested from lower down, nearer the sea bed, and packaged by the same Piran Salt company.

Dario's family has worked these same salt pans for four generations. He bristles with wisdom, and not just about salt farming. "If you want to do good work, you can't be staring at the clock," he says, when I ask what a normal day for him would look like. He works as much as there is work to do, breaking only in the heat of midday. The gathering season requires fine, sunny, hot weather—if there is rain, then there will be no salt to harvest, because the sun will not have been powerful and present enough to burn away the water. So salt, like grains or fruit, is a seasonal harvest. He may work as late as 11:00 p.m., if there is work to be done, a trait he does not see in the periodic farmers brought in to work the pans. "This must be in your blood, because you certainly won't do it for the money."

At the start of Dario's row of six salt pans perches a shack—I want to call it a bungalow, but that would be aggrandizing. It has a narrow covered porch, facing the pans, fitted with a table, where I pause to type up notes. Inside is a wooden bench covered in a simple mattress, a mini fridge with some beverages, a cubbyhole for belongings. This is where Dario can sleep or rest and escape the sun, which is his ally in harvesting, but also an enemy in exhaustion. He uses traditional equipment, as his great-grandfather would have used—likely used for centuries, if not millennia, of Darios, since this very flat has been farmed for sea salt since the time of the ancient Romans. Because the salt crystals are jagged, they can cut bare feet, so some nameless inventor, ages ago, came up with *taperini*, which look like wooden platform flip-flops, the kind of footwear that Venetian courtesans used to wear to keep their dresses above the murk of the aquatic city streets—the proximity of Venice means that this connection may be a direct one. A plank of wood across the soles of the feet rises off the ground thanks to two strips of wood affixed beneath it, like little pontoons. A leather thong atop allows you to slip your feet into it, thus walking atop the salt crystals, protected by the wood. "You've just got to be careful about getting even one crystal stuck between your foot and the thong. That hurts like a bitch," Dario warns with a smile. The broad-brimmed hat and toothless rake are likewise implements of the ancients. The only nod to modernity, if you can call it that, is the set of rail tracks and the very nineteenth century–looking gurney atop it.

——————

Dario points to several rows of salt pans. "That row was my grandfather's. That one my aunt's. That one my father's. We were all *solinarji*, salt farmers." In an average season, Dario can fill up twelve train wagons with salt, for around 240,000 pounds, even 360,000 in a good season. The company expects, as a whole, to process three million pounds of table salt over the course of a season. "If everyone did the same amount of work that I did, then the whole enterprise would make its seasonal quota, and then some," Dario sighs, but they regularly fall short—not enough workers and not enough enthusiasm in the workers they have. This is an unbelievably labor-intensive process, one which I imagine is mechanized elsewhere, but certainly not here. When he's in the groove, and weather permitting, he'll harvest 8,800 to 11,000 pounds a day. That's a lot of raking, shoveling, and gurney-wheeling. And there is a shortage of Darios.

My appreciation for that pinch of salt to top my steak has just increased by some four-to-five-thousand a day.

ADRIATIC TUNA ROULADE WITH KOMBU,
NORI AND RICOTTA, MARINATED CUCUMBER,
GINGER WITH BEETROOT AND TEMPURA,
AND FLEUR DE SEL

DASHI SOUP:

Heat the mineral water, add the kombu kelp, and boil for 10 minutes. Remove the kombu from the liquid, add the bonito flakes, and cook another 7 minutes. Strain the soup and add soy sauce, seasoning with salt if necessary.

2 cups (400 ml) sparkling mineral water
½ sheet kombu kelp
3 tablespoons (40 g) bonito flakes
⅓ cup (80 ml) soy sauce

TUNA:

Freeze the fillet slightly, so that it can be sliced thinly with a meat slicer or mandoline.

About 1 pound (480 g) tuna fillet

KOMBU PURÉE:

Dry-fry the nori for a few seconds on a hot stove, or even on an open flame, until it becomes crisp and the flavor develops. Heat dashi soup in a pan, add the nori, and simmer for approximately 5 minutes. Leave to cool, then blend until smooth. Combine with the ricotta in a food processor and blend to a smooth purée. Season with salt, if necessary, then fill into a piping bag.

10 sheets nori
¾ cup (150 ml) dashi soup
9 ounces (250 g) ricotta
Salt

SPRING ONIONS:

Wash and dry the spring onion leaves, cut into 1¼-inch pieces, and deep-fry until crispy. Place the pieces into dashi soup and cook for about 6 minutes. Transfer everything into a tall container, blend with an immersion blender, and add the xanthan gum, to make a smooth onion purée. Pass through a sieve to make it completely smooth and fill into a piping bag.

7 ounces (200 g) spring onions
Oil for deep-frying
1 cup (200 ml) dashi soup
1 teaspoon (2 g) xanthan gum

GINGER:

Peel the ginger and slice thin with a mandoline. Prepare six containers of boiling water. Dip the ginger slices for 10 seconds in each container, then leave the ginger to cool. This will remove the heat and roughness. Roughly chop the beetroot. Mix water and vinegar, add the beetroot, and cook until the water turns red. Remove the beetroot with a slotted spoon and place the ginger into the red water. Combine the sugar and pectin and add to the beetroot-ginger water. Cook for 15 minutes. Blend to make a red ginger purée.

3½ ounces (100 g) ginger root
1 beetroot
½ cup (100 ml) water
¼ cup (50 ml) apple cider vinegar
1½ tablespoons (20 g) sugar
1 tablespoon (10 g) pectin

MARINATED CUCUMBER:

Slice the cucumber very thin lengthwise using a mandoline, so that the slices are nearly transparent. In a plastic container combine water, sugar, and vinegar to make a marinade. Place the cucumber slices into the marinade. Vacuum three times in a vacuum machine (without a bag).

1 cucumber
1 cup (200 ml) water
3 tablespoons (40 g) sugar
1⅓ tablespoons (20 ml) white vinegar

TEMPURA:

Place the flour, ice, mineral water, and salt in a bowl and whisk gently. Heat the oil to 350°F (175°C). Dip your fingers into the tempura and shake them above the oil, so drops of batter fall in. Fry for a few seconds, then remove tempura balls from the oil with a slotted spoon.

2⅓ ounces (60 g) flour
3 ice cubes
½ cup (100 ml) sparkling mineral water
Salt
Oil for deep-frying

WASABI MARINADE:

Blend dashi soup, olive oil, and wasabi with an immersion blender to make a marinade.

¼ cup (50 ml) dashi soup
2 tablespoons (30 ml) olive oil
1 ounce (30 g) wasabi (freshly grated is best)

TO SERVE:

Slice the tuna into thin slices and arrange them, five in a row. Pipe the kombu purée along the edge of tuna slices and carefully roll into a roulade. Carefully transfer to a plate. Brush the roulade with wasabi marinade, add some ginger purée and spring onion purée. Then add slices of marinated cucumber and tempura balls, and finally decorate with coriander leaves and fleur de sel.

Coriander leaves to decorate
Fleur de sel

MARINATED CORB WITH OLIVE OIL AND FLEUR DE SEL, MARINATED CUCUMBERS, JAPANESE WINEBERRIES, AND LIME SNOW

Fillet the fish, carefully remove all the bones, and cut into ¾-inch pieces. Marinate in olive oil with fleur de sel and keep in the fridge for 2 hours.

About 1 pound (480 g) corb fillets (whole fish 1½ pounds or 700 g)
¼ cup (50 ml) Lisjak olive oil
1½ tablespoons (20 g) fleur de sel

Make a stock using the fish head and bones. First soak the head and bones in cold water for 2 hours, then add the vegetables and rosemary and cook on low heat for 1 hour.

Fish bones and head
Carrot, celeriac, onion, rosemary

CUCUMBER:
Peel and cut the cucumber into ½-inch cubes. Mix the fish stock, olive oil, and salt, seal in a vacuum sealer bag, and cook for 4 minutes in water. Leave to cool. This is best done a day in advance, to ensure that the cucumbers are well-marinated.

1 cucumber
¼ cup (50 ml) fish stock (made from corb bones)
¼ cup (50 ml) olive oil
Salt

LIME SNOW:
Simmer the lime juice and sugar on low heat for 5 minutes, then pour the syrup into a plastic container and freeze. Grate just before serving to make lime snow.

Juice of 4 limes
2 tablespoons (30 g) sugar

TO SERVE:
Place the marinated fish on a plate. Add cucumber cubes with their marinade, the wineberrries, and a little sliced chili. Just before serving, add the lime snow.

32 Japanese wineberries
1 chili

MIRAN BENCETIĆ
AND SARA KOCJANČIČ,
FOGY TARTUFI.
TRUFFLES.

TRUFFLES

—————

"White truffles are like a Dolce and Gabbana or Cartier," says Miran Bencetić. "You breathe in the scent and you just know you're dealing with something special." Miran is the head of Fogy Tartufi, based in Ankaran, on the Slovenian coast. He speaks with precision and passion and enthusiasm and he has reason to be proud. He's the man who sold the world's largest truffle, according to the Guinness Book of World Records. I'll get back to that in a moment. Right now, he is describing how he got started in the truffle business, and how tough it really is.

His phone never stops ringing. He is in touch with 600 to 700 truffle hunters from numerous countries, dotting a very special belt of land that runs through Europe, called the E45 line. It runs from Portugal and Spain across to Italy, through former Yugoslavia to Romania, Moldova, and Bulgaria. This is where the most and the best truffles in the world come from. To be a successful truffle dealer, you have to know not just scores, but hundreds of top truffle hunters throughout this belt. And Miran is one of the best-connected truffle dealers around, with a virtual rolodex of contacts in all of these countries. He has his local hunters, of course, specializing in the Istrian peninsula and the Veneto region of Italy and in Slavonia in northern Croatia, but if there's an exciting find, he will be able to access it, wherever it might come.

He began as a salesman for other foodstuffs. Seafood, sauces, pasta. One day, the company for which he was selling pasta to high-end restaurants gave him a crate with eleven pounds (5 kilos) of black truffles in it. He had eaten truffles but had no deeper experience than that. But he had confidence as a salesman and was up for trying to sell these, as well. He describes the sense of euphoria when he sold that first kilo, and he was hooked. He is a born salesman, conversing convivially with an Italian charm that is not present in all Slovenes, particularly those who live outside of the Primorska region, by the sea. But he has it in spades, and I imagine he would easily be able to sell me even "fried air," as they say around these parts.

But fried air is not on his menu. He sells a lot of black truffles, and today's price, which is set by the European market, is around a $170 per pound (145 euros per kilo). Not too bad, but this is silver to the gold of white truffles. He describes the rarer white varieties as having a much more intense, buttery, and luxurious scent to them, and a price to match. The market price today is approximately $1,800 per two pounds (1,500 euros per kilo), ten times that of their black cousins, and he says that he has seen it go as high as $11,775 (10,000 euros). That's a lot to spend, when you are melting the spendings into your pasta and risotto.

Miran's favorite story is about his Guinness World Record truffle, but he can't tell me the whole tale, at least not on the record. It was the stuff of legend, this *Tuber magnatum pico* that weighed in at a majestic 3,950 pounds (1,786 kilos). Miran has a full-sized model on his desk. It looks like a basketball which has been partially deflated, or some shard of asteroid that crashed to Earth.

When he tells me some of the details, he insists that I pause the recording, as if he is about to tell me some sort of deep dark secret about the Kennedy assassination. Maybe he is. You could do some serious damage with this truffle. The truffle was found by Victoria, one of his favorite truffle hunters, based in central Italy. He grows giddy when he describes her coming across it. "You start digging with a spade in the Earth and you keep seeing more truffle, instead of less. Your heart starts beating more quickly and this sense of elevation comes that makes it feel like you could start floating into the air." Truffle hunting, he says, is a wonderful profession, full of moments of great joy, because it is essentially the work of a professional treasure hunter, digging for edible diamonds in beautiful forests, with canine companions and no clock to punch. But truffle hunters can get emotional, and a bad day or week or month can lead them to a "poisoned state of mind," as he eloquently states. But once you're hooked by the bug, it's hard to quit, because the thrill of the chase remains with you.

As Victoria pulled up this juggernaut truffle, she was delirious with excitement and also not entirely sure what to do with it. She got in touch with Miran, but that was just the start. Miran realized that this truffle bomb would eclipse the current world record in size. He has his network of high-end restaurants and consumers, and they stretch around the world. He will overnight refrigerated boxes to Australia and the United States. But this was too big a find for him to handle by himself. So, he worked with a small consortium, including the major Sabatino Tartufi company, which used six full-time salesmen to promote the record product. It was eventually sold through Sotheby's New York on December 6th, 2014, to . . . well, I'm not allowed to say who bought it, beyond that it went to China for the handsome sum of 61,250 US dollars. For a single (though very large) truffle. It sounds funny to pay so much for something that you are going to shave over your lunch, but once you taste it, you can see why disposable income would be well disposed of in this direction. And if people have paid over one-hundred thousand for a bottle of rare wine that they plan to drink (I'm talking about you, so-called "Jefferson Lafite" bottles), then why not?

I was intrigued to meet Victoria, but she was not available. Another truffle hunter was, however, and she was happy to take us on the hunt through the fungi-rich Istrian forests nearby.

Let it be said, although it may not be politically correct, but the fact that the truffle hunter we are following today—not to mention the one who found the world-record truffle—is a woman is noteworthy, and she is the first to admit it. For whatever reason, the world of truffle hunting has been almost exclusively men's work. There's no good reason for this, no patriarchal tradition or guild system or requirements of brute physical strength. That's just the way it is. Female truffle hunters are few and far between, whereas female mushroom foragers are abundant. Go figure.

We are scampering through an Istrian forest, trailing a pair of handsome dogs. One is a light-colored Labrador, the other a Romagnolo. These are two of the best truffle hunting dog breeds, and part of a pack captained by Sara Kocjančič's family. Puppies are trained from a few weeks old until about six months old, at which time talents as a truffle hunter's assistant become clear.

Full disclosure: I briefly considered training my dog, a Peruvian Hairless named Hubert van Eyck, as a truffle hunter. We were living in Umbria, which is truffle central, and knew of a truffle hunting collective that did dog training. Eyck might have become the first hairless truffle dog. But he's not the brightest bulb in the box, if you know what I mean (the brain is the most overrated organ, anyway), and it didn't happen. But I was curious about how someone less lazy than I could make it happen.

To train your dog to be a truffle hunter, you start by introducing truffle oil poured onto their dog food, when they're just a few weeks old. They start to develop a positive association with it and a taste for it. This is understandable. I would probably be happy to eat dog food if it were covered in truffle oil, too. They then move on to bits of truffle mixed in with their food and then bits of truffle hidden around the garden for them to hunt out. They also play retrieval games, sometimes getting a doggy treat if they retrieve a ball, sometimes a bit of truffle. At the more advanced level, around five months old, entire truffles are hidden buried in the garden for them to sniff out. They must be trained not to gobble them up immediately, because that is their instinct, and even these mature and better-trained truffle hunting dogs will eat the prize, if the hunter doesn't get to them quickly enough and give them a less expensive treat instead.

I had always thought that pigs hunt truffles, and they can, but dogs are considered a better option, despite the fact that pigs are supposedly more intelligent. The main competition for truffles comes in the form of wild boars. It turns out that the scent of truffles is almost identical to the pheromone scent of lady wild boars, so the gentlemen snort around, thinking they are finding a mate and stumble on a delicious truffle to gobble up. They are not very polite about it, and do not cover over the hole after they've dug it up, as human truffle hunters do. This is a problem. You don't want to make it too obvious where one truffle has been found, otherwise other hunters will get there as well.

The best sites for truffles are in oak forests, with a reasonable amount of moisture in the earth, as truffles won't grow if it's too dry. But it is a myth that they only grow at the roots of oak trees. Other trees will welcome them, as well. White truffles grow a few centimeters to a few inches beneath the earth, and therefore are undetectable if you do not have a dog or a pig to scent them. Black truffles, however, grow just below the surface, sometimes even sticking out the tiniest bit. You need laser eyes to find them and an animal, of course, helps tremendously.

After spending time hunting for porcini mushrooms with my enthusiastic and laser-sighted mother-in-law and having seen her find 2¼ pounds (about a kilo) in one session while I found exactly one . . . which turned out to be poisonous . . . I know about the appeal, and potential frustrations, of mushroom hunting. But Sara, during a good season, can find 1 to 2¼ pounds (about a half kilo to a kilo) of white truffles in one day (yes, that can mean over a thousand Euros a day), and black truffles are far more common.

Truffles add an umami, buttery roundness to whatever you add them to: a sauce for a steak, shaved thin with butter and oil over pasta, mixed into risotto, or, the purest way to enjoy them, folded into a light omelet. They can even be used in desserts.

There have been attempts to cultivate them, but it is a risky investment and there is no guarantee that they will take, nor what the yield will be, so it is not considered worth the investment when there are excellent truffle hunters, two-legged and four-, to call upon. Thus, it remains a matter of foraging and forest-traipsing. There is a beauty to the fact that this act has been undertaken by our ancestors dating back as long as is possible to imagine, to our days as hunter-gatherers. There's a communion in this, a sense that good things from the earth that require patience and know-how to find link us to our proto-ancestors. Sophistication aside, from roe deer meat roasted and perhaps rubbed with a truffle over a fire ten-thousand years back to JB's venison medallions with shaved white truffle is not so long a journey, after all.

CREAMED JERUSALEM ARTICHOKE SOUP WITH TRUFFLES, FRIED JERUSALEM ARTICHOKE PEELS, OLIVE OIL, AND RED PEPPERCORNS

Cook the whole Jerusalem artichokes in salted water—25 minutes should suffice, but different tubers may need different cooking times in the same pot. It is better to check several of them and possibly increase cooking time. When soft, halve the artichokes and carefully scoop out the flesh with a small spoon, ensuring that the skin remains as intact as possible. Place the skins on a sheet of baking paper and dehydrate them in a convection oven for 12 hours at 130°F (55°C).

2¼ pounds (1 kg) Jerusalem artichokes

Melt the butter in a saucepan and quickly fry the Jerusalem artichoke flesh. Add the beef and vegetable stocks—the two are used together for a fuller flavor. Add the cream and cook for 10 minutes. Season with salt and mash to make a creamed soup.

3 ounces (80 g) butter
1¼ cups (300 ml) beef stock
1¼ cups (300 ml) vegetable stock
1 cup (200 ml) whipping cream
Salt

Quickly fry the dehydrated artichoke peels: dip into oil for 2 seconds and drain on kitchen paper.

2¼ cups (500 ml) vegetable oil for deep-frying

TO SERVE:
Pour the soup into a bowl. Top with a piece of fried artichoke peel and some thin slices of truffle. Drizzle with a little walnut oil and add some red peppercorns.

1 black truffle, sliced thin
¼ cup (50 ml) walnut oil
Red peppercorns

VEAL SWEETBREADS COATED WITH TRUFFLES, AND CREAM SAUCE WITH TONKA BEAN

———————

VEAL SAUCE:

Bake the veal bones in the oven for about 45 minutes at 375°F (190°C).
In a large pan, fry the roughly chopped onion in oil, then add the roughly chopped vegetables and baked veal bones. Fry a further 15 minutes. Add the beef stock, bay leaf, and peppercorns, and cook, uncovered, on low for 4 hours. Remove from heat, strain, and reduce for a further 2 hours, simmering on a low heat, to obtain a veal sauce.

2¼ pounds (1 kg) veal bones
1 onion
¾ cup (150 ml) sunflower oil
1 carrot
½ celeriac
8½ cups (2 L) beef stock
1 bay leaf
Black peppercorns

CREAM SAUCE:

Simmer the cream on low heat, stirring constantly, until it turns slightly brown and develops a walnut flavor. Then add the grated tonka bean.

1 cup (200 ml) whipping cream
1 tonka bean (1 g) (or 1 g grated vanilla pod)

SWEETBREADS:

Soak the sweetbreads overnight in cold water to clean and rinse. The next day, cook with the carrot, rutabaga, and ½ onion, in salted water on medium heat for 40 minutes. When the sweetbreads are cooked and white, remove the outer membrane, crumble, remove the veins, and finely chop.
Blanch the pork caul fat, remove from the boiling water, and immediately place in cold water.
Heat the oven to 325°F (165°C).
Cut the bread into small pieces. Heat the oil in a saucepan and fry 1 chopped onion until golden brown, then add the sweetbreads and parsley. Fry quickly. Add the pieces of bread, eggs, and herbs. Mix and form into 2-inch balls. Spread out the caul fat and cut into 4-inch squares. Roll the dumplings in the caul fat squares, place onto a tray lined with baking paper, and bake in the oven for 8 minutes.
Cut the truffle into very thin shavings.

¾ pound (400 g) veal sweetbreads
1 carrot
½ small rutabaga
1½ onion, divided
½ cup (100 g) pork caul fat
7 ounces (200 g) white bread
2 sprigs parsley
½ cup (100 ml) vegetable oil
2 eggs
Salt
Pepper
Nutmeg
1 black truffle

TO SERVE:

Place a sweetbread dumpling on a plate, pour veal sauce over it, and coat with the truffle shavings. Use a teaspoon to add some boiled cream to the sauce.

GREGOR LISJAK.
OLIVE OIL.

OLIVE OIL

Olive oil is used so often, and in such quantities, that we don't always think of it in specialist terms. Throughout the Mediterranean it is the basic fat in which we sauté meat and vegetables. We add it to carbohydrates and even consume it by the spoonful for health. Because we use it so regularly, we tend to opt for less expensive bottles, provided they bear the words "extra-virgin" on the label. But beware, because "extra virgins" are not quite as virginal as they used to be.

As a way of benefiting multinational companies that have bought up what appeared to be boutique farm olive oils, regulations in the European Union give to an illogically broad range of quality levels the same label of "extra-virgin." This is like calling anything from 14 to 24 karat gold "pure gold." Technically it may be true, and it is acceptable, legally speaking, but it does not paint the complete picture. There is a wide discrepancy in quality among extra virgin olive oils. The problem is that we consumers see "extra-virgin" and we understand that this is the good stuff, that this is what we want to buy. And then we see one bottle that costs $7 and another that costs $19, and of course we opt for the cheaper one, thinking that it is all the same category, and therefore the same quality. Not so. And while the laws are, at the moment, to the benefit of multinational corporations who can sell oil of a lower quality and still call it "extra-virgin," there are perfectionists out there determined to make the 24-karat version of "extra-virgin" olive oil, and to do it better than the rest.

In Istria, where we are today—just outside the port city of Koper, a few minutes from the Croatian border—there is a limited supply of oil produced. "Everyone who makes good oil here sells out of everything that they make," says Gregor Lisjak, the young, handsome, articulate, dynamic front man of his family's business. He knows his olive oil. As a child, he was obsessed with sailing, but later turned his focus to developing the Lisjak Olive Oil business. He sees the trouble that this broad term "extra-virgin" brings with it. His olive oil is among the most expensive you can find, but there's a reason for it. "Our prices are very high relative to other oils. We cannot compete with quantity, but we compete with quality." The prices here are comparable to those of high-end oil from around Lake Garda—a mecca among olive oil enthusiasts, as opposed to, say, Tuscany, where every farmhouse has their own decent oil in abundance, and prices are low.

Gregor's family business began some thirty years ago, when his father opened an olive mill, *torklja*, to crush olives for the local community, since there were too few mills in the area. He grew olives on his property, but not much more than what was consumed by family and friends, and he also grew all sorts of other produce. During olive season, Gregor's father, Franco, would work as a farmer, while the rest of the year he had a business renting excavators for construction projects. But when Gregor finished his Master's degree in psychology at University of Padua, he and his brother sat down with their father and decided to remake the family's business and branding. They already had years of experience producing what they considered excellent, and pure, extra-virgin olive oil, but they would sell it in bulk, with locals coming by with empty soda bottles to fill up from a tap, and that was that. It was after this family meeting that they determined to hone their product, to bring it to the best level they could, to make a coordinated effort to build up their brand, and to also not just make olive oil generally, but to focus on special varietals of olive trees.

Father Franco took some convincing, because by selling bulk, by December he would sell out of all the oil he could produce, so he considered this a good line of business. But the young brothers managed to sway him into going the extra mile, which meant working on olive oil full-time. This was extra work for the same amount of money that he was already earning part-time by selling bulk, at least for the first few years. But it has paid off. The family plantation has around 1,600 trees now, and each year they still sell out of all they can produce, even at the higher price range. So, they have been planting more trees, at a growth rate of 20 percent more per year, evidence of their astounding success. During the harvest season, which is mid-October to mid-November, depending on the weather, the family works only at the mills, and also buys olives from the neighboring farms, provided they have first pick of the highest quality. They remain small by industrial standards, with nearly 4,000 gallons (15,000 liters) produced in a recent year, so it is small wonder that they sell out, with their bottles on tables of high-end restaurants and discerning family homes throughout Europe.

Theirs is not the sort of olive oil you would use to sauté your onions. You could, of course, but it would be a shame, since the taste is so refined. For cooking purposes, the less expensive olive oils will suffice, and you don't even need them to be extra-virgin to provide a more healthful fat in which to cook. Lisjak's olive oil is for tasting. JB uses it to finish off your dishes, as a final touch, alongside a sprinkling of fleur de sel. It even appears in some of his desserts.

Gregor teaches us to taste olive oil in a special way. There's a particular cup, tulip-shaped and made of cobalt blue glass. It looks like it might hold tea, or a tea light. You pour the oil in, hold it in your palm to warm it gently, allowing it to approach body temperature. Because of the warmth, aromas escape and are directed nose-ward by the tapered opening. "If there are any mistakes in the oil, you can smell it right away," Gregor assures. "The professional tasters don't need to taste to know if it is defective." When tasting, the oil should be swirled around the mouth so it touches all parts of the tongue. "You feel the bitterness in the mouth, spiciness in the throat." You suck in air through your mouth and then through the nose, which enhances the depth of what you taste. The cup is blue because the color is not important and should not distract you. There's an inaccurate prejudice in favor of greener oils over yellow, but Gregor assures us that the color is irrelevant to the taste.

Gregor's olive oil is specifically Istrian. This part of the globe that stretches from Croatia to Italy through Slovenia, is the northernmost swathe where olives can thrive, and they have a distinctive taste from their counterparts at the famous, and southerly, olive oil centers, like Greece or Umbria. But unlike Lake Garda near Milan, which is inland and gets cool breezes from the Alps, Istria is warmed by air from the sea, which keeps the temperature from reaching zero, except in very unusual cases. Winter temperatures are consistently between 32 and 41°F (zero and 5°C) at coldest. This is a striking contrast to just three-quarters of a mile further into Slovenia, where mountains block the sea's warm air and where olive oil is of lesser quality.

The success of Lisjak oil is due to Gregor's understanding and harnessing of his unique location. Trees planted very close to the sea are not that good for olives. The best soil is in the hills, away from the ocean, but kissed by sea winds. The higher the hill, the better the tree. Then there are micro-locations. "We plant our trees just where, hundreds of years ago, olive trees were planted," Gregor explains. "You can plant olive trees or grapes for wine anywhere. You just need water and fertilizer. But if you take these ingredients away, if you stop feeding the plants, then they will die. If you plant them where the plants have always been, then they will live and thrive, even without human intervention."

Because, in former Yugoslavia, there was no rich tradition of using olive oil, people from the area who wanted to learn about olives looked abroad. This is also one of the few negative Slovenian tendencies–to give precedence and greater respect to just about anything from abroad, over the homegrown. It's starting to change, but it hints at an inferiority complex. The Spanish, the Italian, the Greek system for olive oil must be better than the Slovenian one, many locals would instinctively think. But not so, or at least not for growing olives in Slovenian lands. "Everyone you ask for advice will tell you that their methods and olive varietals are best. So, Slovenians were going to Italy, to Greece, and bringing back plants and knowledge and planting them here," Gregor explains. "We experimented with many Mediterranean varieties, but also our Istrian varieties in the same soil, on our land. It turned out that Istrian varieties are more aromatic, spicy, bitter–everything is a step ahead of the other varieties. At least when grown in our lands. It's like with wine. Cabernet, planted in France or in Italy or in special regions in France, will taste different." But the best of all is what is most natural, whatever is indigenous to the region. This is the Tao of Olive Oil—keeping in step with Nature's will.

"Old Istrian varieties are the best for Istrian locations." Buga, Istrska Belica, Storta, Drobnica, Črnica . . . there are twelve indigenous Istrian varietals in all. Lisjak produces a single origin Istrska Belica (Istrian White) that is the star of their lineup. They offer a mix of Mediterranean varietals, which is sweeter, less bitter, but also less complex, more of an everyday oil, for salads, risotto, pasta. The next we taste is a mixture, but of many Istrian varietals only. Totally local. This one has more subtlety to it, and Gregor and JB both agree that it's best served in the simplest way possible, as one of three components to a meal—fresh fish, fleur de sel, and good oil. That's all you need for the perfect Mediterranean plate.

The lesson is to grow local and taste what is local. But what interests me most is what is hyper-local, found only in one place. Tastes that are not only worth a journey, but which *require* a journey. When it comes to olive oil, taste blind, suck in air as you roll it over your tongue and taste local/regional varietals where they've always grown. When in Istria, Istrian White is where it's at.

HAZELNUT ICE CREAM
WITH OLIVE OIL,
DARK CHOCOLATE,
AND FLEUR DE SEL

PRALINE:

Place the sugar into a saucepan and heat to make dark caramel. When it begins to foam, add the hazelnuts and stir quickly but thoroughly, so that the hazelnuts are well-coated. Immediately spread onto a silicone tray and leave to cool completely. Grind the cooled hazelnuts in a food processor or Thermomix to make a spreadable paste.

½ cup (100 g) sugar
10½ ounces (300 g) toasted skinned hazelnuts

ICE CREAM:

Heat the milk and sugar to approximately 175°F (80°C). The sugar should dissolve completely. Stir in the hazelnut praline, transfer to a Pacojet beaker or ice cream maker, and freeze for 24 hours. (Alternatively, if an ice cream machine is not available, transfer to a plastic container and freeze. Break or cut into smaller pieces, then blend with an immersion blender until smooth.)

2 cups (400 ml) milk
¼ cup + 2 tablespoons (80 g) sugar
14 ounces (400 g) hazelnut praline

Melt the chocolate with the olive oil in a double boiler until it is shiny and smooth.

1 ounce (30 g) dark chocolate (75% cocoa)
1 teaspoon (5 g) olive oil

TO SERVE:

For each serving, pour 2 tablespoons (30 ml) extra virgin olive oil into a cocktail glass (a milder tasting oil is preferred), place a scoop of ice cream over the oil, and pour the chocolate sauce over the top. Finish with a sprinkling of fleur de sel.

½ cup (120 ml) mild olive oil, divided
Fleur de sel

NOTE:

This recipe makes enough ice cream for at least 20 scoops. The ice cream can be stored in an airtight container in the freezer for up to a month.

POURED NOODLES
WITH RED SAUCE
AND MUSSELS

NOODLES:

Whisk the egg, yolk, flour, salt, chopped sage, and olive oil in a bowl until smooth. The batter should be rather thick — add a little flour if necessary. Fill the batter in a piping bag, make a small hole, and pipe into boiling salted water in a thin stream. Cook the noodles for 5 minutes, remove with a slotted spoon, cool in a bowl of cold water, and drain.

1 egg
1 egg yolk
½ cup (100 g) 00 flour
Salt
3 sage leaves
¼ cup (50 ml) olive oil

RED SAUCE:

Cut a cross shape into the stem end of the tomatoes for easy peeling and blanch them in boiling water. Remove the skins and chop the tomatoes.
Chop the shallots and fry them in the olive oil with the sugar, until translucent. Add the tomatoes and finely chopped garlic, cover, and braise for 20 minutes on low. Stir occasionally. Finally, season with salt and pepper and blend with an immersion blender to make a smooth purée.

1 ounce (30 g) ripe plum tomatoes
½ cup (100 ml) olive oil
½ cup (100 g) shallots
2 tablespoons (30 g) sugar
2 cloves garlic, finely chopped
Salt and pepper

SHELLFISH STOCK:

Pour a bit of olive oil into a pot and add the mussels and scallops. Cover and cook until the shells open, about 5 minutes, then remove from the pot and remove the flesh from the shells. Set the flesh aside and return the shells to the pot together with the roughly chopped shallots. Add the juice of the orange, as well as thin strips of zest, peeled and sliced ginger, bay leaf, and carrot, and fry for 10 minutes. Then add the ice cubes to the pot to draw even more flavor out of the shells. Cook a further 20 minutes and strain to obtain a shellfish stock. There will only be a few tablespoons of the stock.

2¼ pounds (1 kg) mussels
28 small scallops
Water remaining from cooking the shellfish
2 shallots
½ orange
1½ tablespoons (20 g) ginger root, peeled and sliced
1 bay leaf
½ carrot
6 ice cubes

TO SERVE:

Pour the tomato sauce into a saucepan, add the shellfish flesh and stock, and cook on low heat for 5 minutes. Heat the noodles quickly in boiling water, then drain and add them to the saucepan. Stir well and arrange on a plate. Drizzle with olive oil if desired.

Olive oil to drizzle (optional)

ALES WINKLER,
KUMPARIČKA GOAT FARM.
GOAT CHEESE.

GOAT CHEESE

Nothing says "Welcome to my farm" like a skull impaled on a stick. And when it's a goat farm, well, naturally the skull should be from an ex-goat. We'd been driving for hours, and while technically we were only twenty minutes from Pula, the largest city in the Istrian peninsula, it sure felt like we were in the middle of nowhere. Where better to find what is considered one of the best goat cheese producers in the world? It was adventure enough to follow unhelpful but optimistic signs for Kumparička, the name of the farm (it sounds just as weird to Slovenes as it does to foreigners). There were signs dotted around the nearest town, depicting a smiling goat and the name of the farm (and its Facebook page!) but without directions or even an arrow to aim us appropriately. Good thing I had a copilot, my Mexican writer buddy, Carlos. To tell you the one about the American and the Mexican looking for a Slovenian goat farmer in Croatia sounds like a joke, but it's a good thing I had a wing man with me. JB and Matjaž drove down separately, and this was a lot of driving (at least by Slovenia-sized standards, where you can't really drive more than two hours and still be in the country), and it would also be a lot of eating, by any standards.

Passing the impaled goat skull, which appeared to be smiling, we wound our way down a very long drive, flanked by ancient, crumbling stone walls and vast fields of what the locals call *makija*, from the Italian *macchia* for "stain" (if that doesn't ring a bell, then recall *café macchiato*, which means a coffee with a little "stain" of milk, or *Madonna Immaculata*, which describes the Virgin Mary "unstained" by sin). The local version of *makija* is scrubland: dry fields pocked with patches of grass, the occasional torqued tree, earth more scorched than lush, but still with sufficient rain, and access to the sea winds, to be alive with flora and fauna. In short, this is goat heaven.

My buddy Carlos and I pulled up in front of a series of low-slung outbuildings that look more hacienda than working farm, much less award-winning goat-cheesery. Having gotten sufficiently lost, we're a half hour behind Matjaž and JB, who are over at the goat pen. We're told to wait outside, because the Maremma sheepdogs might otherwise attack. Apparently there's a little problem with coyotes. Coyotes? Carlos and I both thought we'd misheard. We associate coyotes with the prairies in his Mexico and my America. Turns out there are, indeed, European coyotes, and they've developed a taste for goat. A gaggle of twelve enthusiastic dogs, goat bodyguards, rush toward us, called to a halt by the master goatier, Aleš Winkler.

Let me say this right from the start. Winkler is all kinds of cool. The coolest guy we've encountered on our travels. Someone I immediately clicked with and would happily visit regularly for beers and rolled cigarettes, even if he did not offer the finest goat cheese this side of the Pyrenees. He rocks up in oversized pajama-like pants, an unfashionably ripped t-shirt, a smile on his face, and the eyes of a man whose cares were left at his previous port of call. Aside from the occasional errant coyote, life is good.

Let it be said that Aleš Winkler is not un-goat-like in appearance. Wily, laughing eyes, unshaven, whiskery visage, shaggy hair. He's entirely aware of this and, unlike most Slovenes, he has a very good sense of humor about himself. His phone's ring tone is a goat bleating. The staff on his farm wear t-shirts emblazoned with the words "No goats no glory." I make a mental note to ask for one of the t-shirts.

Winkler is the worldliest farmer you're likely to come across. When Matjaž asks him to lift one of the young goats and carry him across his shoulders, for a photograph, he immediately recognizes the visual reference that I, as an art history professor, see: the photo recalls Caravaggio's painting of *Saint John the Baptist,* who is likewise depicted as draped in goat. Winkler even knows that the model for Caravaggio's Saint John, Cecco da Caravaggio, was referred to as the "goat-faced boy" for his physiognomic resemblance to the aforementioned quadruped.

Educated in Ljubljana and having worked as one of Slovenia's top real estate lawyers, Winkler took what might, for some, have been a midlife crisis and transmuted it into a shift for the better. "You know how it is," he begins. "When you're twenty, you don't know what will happen when you're thirty. When you're thirty, you're not sure about your forties. But when you're forty, you have a good idea where life is going. So it was a good time to stop the moment and count again. I've had two lives in one!"

Winkler's decision to shift from law to goats he describes as "organic." "I found the property first, to use it like a vacation house. I was thinking of whether to move from a flat in Ljubljana to a house in Ljubljana, or to buy this estate. It was a good decision." Winkler had his property cleared with mulchers, to get rid of the scrub and make the land more user-friendly. "But within a year, it came back, much worse than before!" There was no tradition of having goats in the area, aside from a family keeping a single goat here and there for milk and cheese. "Shitty cheese," Winkler clarifies. "They made much better cheese from sheep milk, because this is much easier to make. So people here had this idea that goat cheese is not good, so why have goats?" Winkler first bought thirty goats, not for the cheese, but as lawnmowers. They found a farmer to hire to care for them. But now they had a full-time goat farmer, but only thirty goats-as-fuzzy-lawnmowers. "The guy said, come on, bring me more goats!" So they bought another hundred. Then came the inevitable question: what to do with all the milk that they produce? "I thought, what the hell, really?" Winkler hadn't calculated the necessity to milk his lawnmowers. "So we start milking, but nobody wanted to buy the milk! Professional cheesemakers wanted to buy at least five hundred liters from us, and we didn't have that much." So Winkler took matters into his own hands. "I studied for a year. I went on the internet and bought every book on Amazon about goat cheese. After that we started making cheese. The first year, it was really shit. The second year, we were champions of Croatia." The man boasts a quick learning curve. "If you recognize the mistakes, it's very easy. You mustn't be a farmer," says the farmer. "You must think different."

Goats and goat cheese have never been appreciated in Slovenia the way they are in France, where goat cheese is expensive and important. You can find it, but the aged, hard cheese, not the creamy pyramids, coated in pepper or ashes or, as in Winkler's case, saffron. For Slovenes goats are gardeners rather than lunch providers, and this makes Winkler's project even more unusual. Actually it is an innovative improvement, taking an animal (goat), which is common on the farms, and using its product (milk), which most Slovenes don't care much about. With the quality of his products he creates a new culinary tradition, opening people's eyes and inspiring them. Following his success, more farms in Slovenia and Istria took up production of top-quality goat cheese. But they will not easily achieve similar results.

Winkler is clearly having fun with this whole farming thing. For instance, he uses drones to keep track of his goats, as they munch their way across his 620 acres (250 hectares) of scrub. It makes shepherding more like a video game, as he sits with his beer at home and follows the herd by remote control to locate a stray, but it's even more effective. "The goats are afraid of the drones," he says, "so you can even herd them in the right direction by flying the drones around. But mostly it's fun." Winkler shows us his cheese cave, impeccable and the only part of the farm that is off-limits to his anti-coyote army of dogs. Its light-controlled, viewable through glass from a mezzanine balcony, wooden planks stacked into the sky, bearing his award-winning discs of goaty goodness. His product is so highly considered that he is ranked, already, among the best in Europe. The year we visited him, 2017, he was the invited guest at Slow Food International in Turin, where he taught the French and Italians a thing or two about making goat cheese. It's been a wild ride.

The rough wooden table in his open-air kitchen/lounge/dining room bears a bowl of what looks like tropical fruit. Turns out its tomatoes, but not as I know them. There's not a shape or color that is familiar to me from the supermarket. The sizes range from teardrop to fist, a wash of yellow and purple and green and mauve. All from his garden. They taste more like plums, kiwis, cucumbers, mangos, than tomatoes. This is a whole new ballgame. But aren't we here for the cheese? This would be a destination just for the tomatoes.

And out they come. Three levels of ageing for the hard cheeses, but I'm most intrigued by the soft ones. I grew up enjoying a rather industrial, but still tasty, version of goat cheese in peppercorns or herbs, from the local supermarket. This is at another level of succulence, intensity, goat-i-ness. Slovenia is a land unbothered by raw dairy. Pasteurization is not necessary. It sounds funny to them to learn that, in America, you can buy assault weapons, but not unpasteurized milk. That there are, right now, people in prison for selling raw dairy products. The rawness of milk or cheese means that the taste is so much fuller, more natural, bearing the essence of the vessel (in this case, happy lady goats) which carried its ingredient, and even a trace of whatever that vessel ate (in this case, the wild grasses of the Istrian *makija*). Winkler's most-awarded cheese is a soft one imbued with saffron. Sliced open, the inside is a custard-yellow, beautiful to behold. But I'm most intrigued with the hairy one. Cheese, one would think, is not meant to be hairy. I've heard tell that the hairy "silken tofu," a specialty in some parts of China, is a very much acquired taste, and would not be my thing. Now Winkler proudly serves us a column of goat cheese that appears to be sheathed in gray felt. It looks alarmingly like a pair of winter slippers I have back at the house. Slicing into it, there's a surprise, as well–a thin orange layer just beneath the gray felt exterior and soft white insides. But it does not taste anything like my slipper. This is the one, the big gun. I can't get enough of it.

In his restaurant JB serves Winkler's cheese on its own, because he is proud to present the noblest raw ingredients as they are, as part of a cheese platter, maybe with some damson chutney, but that's it. He also incorporates it into dishes, for example a play of hot and cold in a bowl of fresh pasta. "I use Winkler's goat ricotta cold in an otherwise hot dish of pasta with cherry tomatoes and celeriac sauce," explains JB. Cold cheese and hot pasta mingle in every bite; they play with your mind, your tongue becoming a playground. Winkler's hard, mature cheese gives an exciting salty-meaty note to JB's gnocchi, accompanying beef, and brings the meat and the side dish into balance as a leit-motif.

In 2016, Winkler opened a *konoba*, Croatian for an informal restaurant, like the Italian *osteria*, but he does it his way. It's clear from the sign at the entrance, which reads *konoba Primitiva*, which means just what you'd think it does. A chalkboard lists the "rules:" 1) Animal welfare (presumably up until the moment said animal is transformed from noble beast into dinner), 2) Self-service is good for you, 3) Smile and talk, and 4) is left blank, for you to fill in from the basket of chalk hanging beside the chalkboard. The konoba opens at 7:00 p.m. If you're not there then, tough noogies. They serve you whatever they made that day. And it's killer good. Winkler and his son do the serving. No plates, just rustic wooden cutting boards spread with ridiculously delicious, fresh things (think Croatian/Slovenian tapas, lots of small servings of vegetables, spreads, cheeses, sausages), to be eaten by spoon or by hand or spread with the inevitable Bowie-sized knife that is stuck upright in the cutting board. Instead of plates, flatbreads studded with rosemary, roasted garlic, and tomatoes, the span and shape of flying saucers, are thumped onto the table. The beer is cold, the cheese is goaty, vocal jazz spins out of a speaker that hangs from a rafter, fairy lights string above the few communal tables. Life is good.

Come 8:00 p.m., service ends. You can stay as long as you like, grab that guitar or the accordion from the pile next to the beer cooler, but Winkler and his family have better things to do than cater to you. It's a good life. One might even say, with a measure of objectivity, that it's a better quality of life than being a high-rolling real estate lawyer in the big city. Winkler certainly seems the better for it. So grab another beer, roll a cigarette, then roll a roll of Europe's best goat cheese in a bowl of pulverized black peppercorns. Uproot the Bowie knife from its wooden board, hack off a wedge of flatbread, and go to town. But only metaphorically. You're already in the best place on earth.

HOMEMADE MACARONI
IN TOMATO SAUCE WITH
GOAT RICOTTA AND CELERY

PASTA:

Mix flour, yolks, and salt to make pasta dough.
If too thick, add a tablespoon of water. Knead
for 10 minutes. Place the dough in a bowl,
cover with cling film, and put into the fridge
to rest for half an hour. Then use a pasta
machine to make macaroni shapes. Cut them
to a length of approximately ¾-inch. If you
don't have pasta machine with a macaroni
attachment, make tagliatelle. The pasta may
be cooked immediately or spread onto a tray
to dry.

Cook the pasta in salted water for 16 minutes
(or 8 minutes for tagliatelle). Drain, but
reserve some of the cooking water.

5¼ ounces (150 g) flour
6 egg yolks
Salt

TOMATO SAUCE:

Blanch and peel the tomatoes. Roughly chop
and place into a sieve so that some of the
juice drains off. Reserve the juice.

Pour the reserved tomato juice into a sauce
pan, add the agar agar, and heat to 185°F
(85°C). Pour onto a silicone tray ½-inch thick
and chill for 2 hours to set. When set and cool,
cut it into cubes.

Sauté the chopped onion in the olive oil until
softened, then add the chopped tomato, salt,
and sugar. Cook a further 12 minutes, adding
a little of the pasta water.

When the sauce is cooked, add the pasta and
cook another 5 minutes.

About ¾ pound (400 g) ripe oxheart tomatoes
½ teaspoon (2 g) agar agar
1 onion, chopped
½ cup (100 ml) olive oil
1½ tablespoons (20 g) sugar

Clean the celery, cut into long pieces, and
blanch for 2 minutes, then sauté in olive oil.

¼ pound (120 g) celery

TO SERVE:

Place the pasta and sauce in a bowl, arrange
the ricotta cheese around it, and top with the
cubes of tomato jelly and sautéed celery.

5¼ ounces (150 g) goat ricotta

RAVIOLI WITH PISTACHIOS AND RICOTTA, PEAR PURÉE, FOIE GRAS, AND VEAL AND CREAM SAUCE

Combine the flour, yolks, and salt and knead to form a dough. Leave to rest for half an hour at room temperature.

3½ ounces (100 g) 00 flour
4 egg yolks
Salt

For the filling, finely chop the pistachios, then blend in a food processor or Thermomix with the ricotta, salt, and pepper until smooth. Simmer the fresh cream on low heat until it turns slightly brown and develops a nutty aroma.

¼ cup + 2 tablespoons (80 g) green pistachios
5¼ ounces (150 g) goat ricotta
Salt
Pepper
1 cup (200 ml) whipping cream

Core the pears, cut into quarters, toss with sugar and olive oil, and bake for 15 minutes at 340°F (170°C). Process the baked pears to make a purée.

7 ounces (200 g) Williams pears
3½ tablespoons (50 g) brown sugar
¼ cup (50 ml) olive oil

Mix the licorice with the milk, seal it into a vacuum sealer bag, then place into a water bath (sous-vide) for 2 hours at 175°F (80°C). Take it out of the water bath, but leave in the bag, and leave overnight to allow the flavor to develop.

1 ounce (30 g) licorice powder
1 cup (200 ml) milk

Roll the dough thin and cut out 2- to 2¼-inch circles. Place a spoon of pistachio filling in the middle, fold the dough to make ravioli, and seal the edges. Cook for 10 minutes in salted water.

TO SERVE:
Warm the licorice milk and blend with an immersion blender to make froth.
Sauté the cooked ravioli in butter and arrange on a plate. Pour the cream and veal stock over the ravioli. Add the pear purée, licorice froth, and slices of fresh foie gras, seasoned with fleur de sel.

3½ tablespoons (50 g) butter
1 cup (200 ml) good-quality veal stock
3½ ounces (100 g) foie gras
Fleur de sel

JOŠKO SIRK.
WINE VINEGAR.

WINE VINEGAR

When was the last time you thought, I mean really thought deeply, about vinegar? Approximately never? Yeah, that was my answer, too. But there are those who have set aside years of their lives to its study, and it turns out that they are onto something. One such man is Joško Sirk.

Sirk straddles Slovenia and Italy, literally and figuratively. His renowned restaurant, Trattoria al Cacciatore della Subida, which carries a Michelin star, is the flagship, and it can be found in Italy, but just a few minutes' drive across the border from Slovenia. The chef is his son-in-law, and La Subida has become a miniature empire of relaxation, a stretch of wooded landscape sprawling over many acres, dotted with unique cottages for rental, including a clutch of them that form a sort of miniature village, woven through with nature trails. This is the place to take your sweetheart, with a secluded aura to it. There is more than one restaurant on the premises, with a less formal osteria joyously decorated in hunting trophies, elaborately-antlered deer skulls (Sirk is an avid hunter), but which have been painted in lively pastel colors.

Sirk inherited the restaurant at age sixteen, when his father died unexpectedly. From that point on, he was the main breadwinner in the family, caring for his sisters, and he has not looked back since. Sirk wears the subtle moustache and the charming smile of a 1930s Hollywood matinee idol. He is known, à la Tom Wolfe, for always wearing a white linen suit. But what really distinguishes him is that he has spent his post-chef years obsessing about vinegar.

I'm a fan of balsamic vinegar, the really good kind that tastes like liquefied raspberries. I like apple cider vinegar and have heard of its medicinal properties–I drink a glass of water containing a drop of cider vinegar when I wake each morning, for reasons I've never understood but are something to do with making me live longer. But this is neither. Sirk's vinegar is made of grapes, the finest he can find, not the dregs and skins and stems that are often used while the good grapes go for wine. What Americans tend to call wine vinegar gets short shrift, but it turns out that we're missing out.

Balsamic vinegar is a different thing. It's a specialty of Emilia-Romagna, with its own important culture, and a different base from the wine vinegar Sirk makes. Balsamic vinegar is cooked fermented grape juice, to break it down to its basics, so it has a lot more sugar retained than Sirk's uncooked wine vinegar. They are different end results, with the common origin as products of fermented grapes. The best balsamic vinegars take a lot of time to mature, decades, even up to a century in some cases. But the vast majority of balsamic vinegars available are industrially-produced and chemically "aged." Balsamic vinegar is great but must be considered distinct from what Sirk is so passionate about.

Historically, vinegar was one of the only known antiseptics, and so had a medicinal role. It was likewise one of the only preservatives for food, when salt was in short supply or entirely unavailable, Sirk explains. Today, he continues, every human on earth could do with a dose of vinegar every day, as it helps our bodies regulate digestion. But over the last century or so, the quality of the vinegar the world consumes dropped dramatically. It is the result of cutting corners–vinegar was once made of prime ingredients, but then it was side-lined and only grape skins, stems, and outcast grapes were made into vinegar. With a few friends, Sirk is on a crusade to bring back the lost quality. He founded *Amici Acidi*, Vinegar Friends, a team of four close friends from the food and wine world, who each produce vinegar the traditional way, and champion its use.

Italy is the biggest exporter of vinegar, with 500 million or so bottles produced per year. But of all that quantity, only 15 producers in all of Italy make vinegar the old-fashioned way, using only the best ingredients, he says, and together they produce far less than 1 percent of the total amount made in Italy. None of them make a living off of their vinegar production—all do it out of passion for tradition, culture, and food.

Direct from the vines, Sirk brings grapes to ferment in huge vats, with the sugar in the grapes converting into alcohol. This newer product is mixed with the previous year's vinegar and the two mingle for approximately one year, souring the mixture to the appropriate measure. The product is decanted, then this cocktail sits in wooden barriques for around two years, until it mellows to Sirk's taste. Then it is bottled in dark glass.

Sirk's "cellar" is actually a wooden barn with wide steps sloping down a hill. Each step contains a line of wooden barrels. It looks like a whiskey or wine cellar. Though the scale appears grand, Sirk only produces around 10,000 bottles a year.

Sirk's vinegar comes in a slim spray bottle, and a little goes a long way. A spray or two to top off just about anything you're eating is a welcome addition to, well, anything. Wherever Sirk finds a fat (butter, oil, lard), he sprays some of his vinegar to cut it. "That's the game," Sirk says. He uses it in two ways. First, as a main complimentary ingredient to dishes, improving the taste, of course, but also helping us to digest it. Sirk uses it to prepare sausage, oily fish, in marinades, in *jota* (a traditionally Slovenian sauerkraut or sour turnip stew), in bean dishes, and much more. The second way is as a grace note to a finished dish, like eggs or risotto. This is why you'll find a slender bottle of his vinegar on every table of his restaurant, to spray a single spritz atop a dish, the way you might add a pinch of salt or a dash of the finest olive oil. "Vinegar adds freshness to anything," Sirk emphasizes.

While Sirk swears by vinegar, not only for taste, but also for digestive health, the taste is reason enough for me. If it helps my digestion, well, I consider that a bonus. Once I've been introduced to this wonder, I find myself spraying it on anything I can get my hands on, even odd options, like *kaisersmarrn*, the Austrian shredded pancake, and a recent bowl of cream of mushroom soup. It really does suit, everywhere. Best to keep a bottle in your purse at all times.

If you can swing by La Subida, you'll want to try the vinegar ice cream, an effervescent, lighter-than-air sorbet that feels like it could make you float.

MARINATED KVARNER MACKEREL WITH VINEGAR, TOMATO PURÉE, BLACK OLIVE POWDER, AND SAMPHIRE

BLACK OLIVE POWDER:

Pit the olives, add the crumbled bread, ink, and salt and knead well. Make small piles of the mixture and dry in a dehydrator for approximately 8 hours. When completely dry, grind to a powder in a coffee grinder.

2 ounces (60 g) black olives
1½ ounces (40 g) white bread, crust removed, crumbled
1 teaspoon squid ink
Salt

MACKEREL:

Clean the mackerel, wash, pat dry with a cloth, and make a shallow cut lengthwise. Heat olive oil in a pan and fry the fish approximately 2 minutes on each side. Remove the cooked fish from the pan and keep warm.
Place the vinegar, water, lemon juice, and ginger into the pan used to cook the fish. Stir quickly and remove from the heat. Place the mackerel into the sauce, cover the pan, and leave to cool.

8 fresh mackerel (2¼ pounds or 1 kg)
½ cup (100 ml) olive oil
2 tablespoons (30 ml) Sirk vinegar
½ cup (100 ml) water
Juice of ½ lemon
1½ tablespoons (20 g) grated fresh ginger root

TOMATO PURÉE:

Blanch the tomatoes, peel, and cut into small pieces. Heat the oil and sugar in a saucepan and cook for 2 minutes, then add the finely chopped onion, fry quickly, and stir in the tomato. Season with salt and pepper, cover the pan, and braise for 10 minutes, stirring frequently. When cooked, blend with an immersion blender to make a purée. Leave to cool.

2 ripe tomatoes
½ cup (100 ml) olive oil
1 teaspoon sugar
½ onion, finely chopped
Salt
Pepper

Quickly fry the samphire in a few drops of olive oil.

Rock samphire
Olive oil

TO SERVE:

Place the fish on a plate and spread sauce from the pan over the top. Season with some fleur de sel, add tomato purée and samphire, finally sprinkling with the olive powder.

Fleur de sel

SORBET OF GREEN APPLE, LIME, AND BASIL WITH WINE VINEGAR

Soak the gelatin in cold water to soften. Core the apples and cut them into small pieces, and roughly chop the basil, including the stems.

Boil the mineral water with the sugar and add the apples, lime juice, basil, and squeezed out gelatin. Blend with an immersion blender, transfer to a Pacojet beaker or ice cream maker, and freeze.

If an ice cream machine is not available, place the sorbet in a plastic container and freeze. Break or cut the sorbet into smaller pieces, then blend with an immersion blender until smooth.

TO SERVE:
Scoop the sorbet into a cold bowl or plate and add two or three sprays of vinegar.

12 teaspoons Knox gelatin powder (12 leaves gelatin)
7 Granny Smith apples
7 ounces (200 g) basil
4¼ cups (1 L) mineral or other sparkling water
14 ounces (400 g) sugar
2 cups (400 ml) lime juice

Sirk wine vinegar in a spray bottle

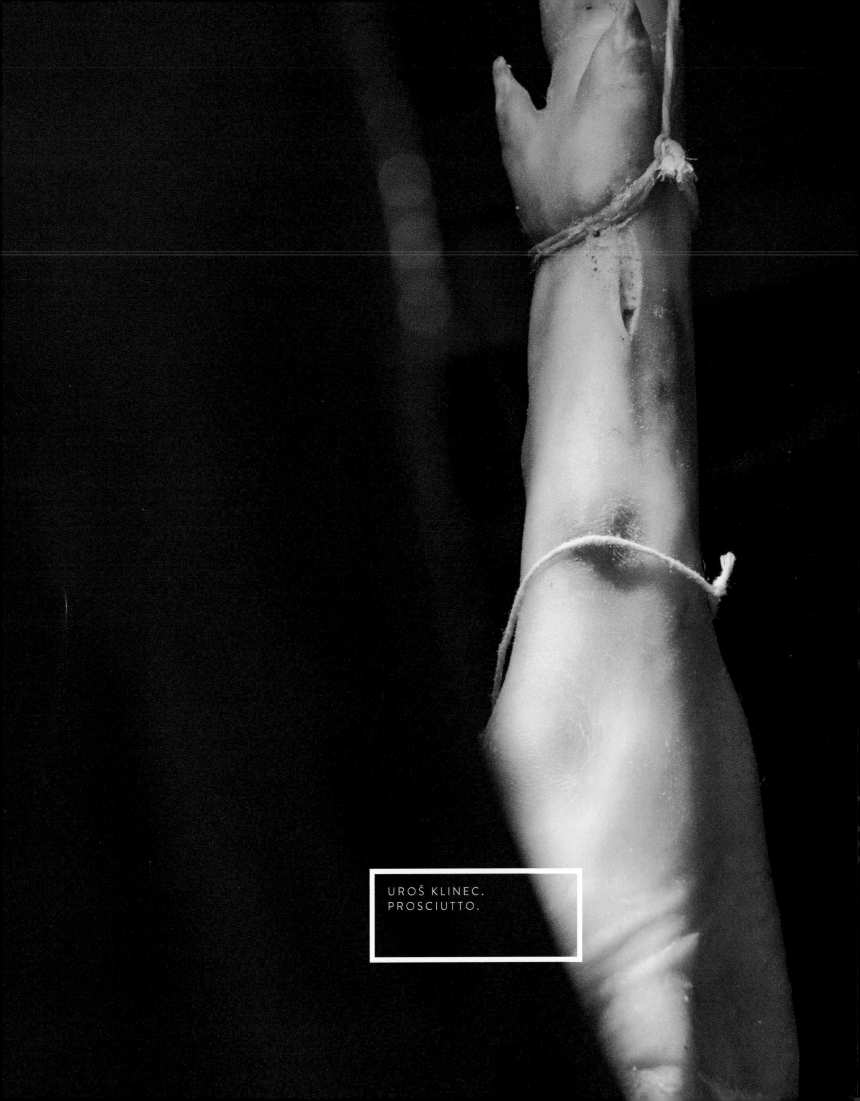

UROŠ KLINEC.
PROSCIUTTO.

PROSCIUTTO

If the idea of being buried alive in a sea of aged pig legs sounds like a nightmare, then this is not the place for you. If, on the other hand, you are like me, and think that pork is perhaps God's greatest invention, then this is a dimly-lit, Caravaggesque slice of heaven. I'm standing in the midst of a porcine corridor. Left and right, running the length of the row—one of many—hang hind legs of Krško polje, or Blackstrap pigs, an indigenous breed that has the perfect fat quotient for making prosciutto, what the Slovenes call *pršut*. It strikes me that, were I vegetarian or Muslim (or especially a Muslim vegetarian), then this would qualify as a circle of hell. As I am neither, I feel like I've found Shangri-La.

Matjaž is partial to heavy chiaroscuro in his photos, picking out spotlights that bring his subject forward from the inky murk. The single light in this drying room, buried behind the *agriturismo* run by Uroš Klinec and his wife, Nejka, already provides the sort of light that Caravaggio made famous. Matjaž is in his element, as he snaps away at Uroš, whose spiky hair nicely echoes the punk rock stylings of the remaining fur on a leg of wild boar, which is hidden amongst the hairless and waxen Krško polje pig legs on display. They are aged at least two years, and up to as many as four. Stored in a room with a constant 75 percent humidity, Uroš ages his pršut in a damper and more enclosed space than most producers. The *burja* (Bora) wind works its magic, but not with constant gusts, more with atmospheric saturation. His pršut is silken, ⅗ pure white fat striping the bottom, ⅖ perfect, evenly-colored pink muscle. "Great pršut must melt in your mouth," JB whispers, so as not to interrupt Matjaž's flow. "If you have to chew it, you already know it's no good."

There's a catch about this, and indeed many of the producers from whom JB buys his ingredients. He considers this the best pršut in the world. At the same level, if not better, than the top producers of *pata negra*, San Daniele, Parma D.O.P. and the other fine purveyors of air-dryed pig legs of the world. But you cannot buy it.

Well, that's not entirely true. If you come here, to Uroš's farm, you can buy it. If you phone him up and are just a drive away–in Milan or Bologna or Vienna or Ljubljana–then you can. But it is very expensive. And it is very rare. And Uroš has to want to sell it to you, which is not a given. Uroš makes precisely eighty legs a year, no more. He makes an even smaller amount of salami, pancetta, rolled pancetta, and a handful of other products that mean he uses every part of the pig. That includes the trotters, in case you were wondering. "A Japanese company wanted to order my pršut," Uroš confides, "but insisted that the trotters be removed, because Japanese customers wouldn't want pršut carved at their table if the pig's leg looks too much like, well, a pig's leg. I said, 'No. If my pigs arrived with trotters on, they'll go out with trotters on!'" He smiles, broadly and with a warmth that I associate with Italians. No surprise, as you could quite literally throw a stone over to the Italian border. This village, adjacent to the famous center for wine and cherries, Goriška brda, hosts a cluster of the finest Slovenian wine producers: Ščurek, Movia, Belica, Simčič. Half of them have their vines on the Slovenian side of the border, half over in Italy.

So even if you want to buy one of his pršut legs, even if you offer a barrow-full of money, you might not be able to buy it. He sells out all he makes, and doesn't want to make more. "I want to keep this fun, keep it my passion," he says. To expand would feel like work. He names his price, he sells out, and he sells to those to whom he wants to sell, primarily five-star hotels and Michelin-starred, or Michelin-quality, restaurants. "And I have to keep enough for the family, otherwise they get mad at me," he jokes. He is fastidious. The entry to his pršut sanctuary has a double set of doors. He closes one as we pass through it and checks, very carefully, for any insects that might have followed us. Only when the coast is clear do we proceed through the second door. "A single fly can cause all sorts of problems," he says. "This would be fly heaven."

Each leg of pršut loses 25 percent of its mass during the drying process. It begins with the hind quarters of the pigs. Uroš carefully chooses not only the breed of pig (he prefers local Krško polje pig or the Hungarian indigenous Mangalica, the two that Primož Krišelj, whom we'll meet in a later chapter, raises on his farm), but the individual pigs, themselves. It's a luxury he can afford because of the small quantity, which means the quality is exceptional. His pršut legs cost twice as much as other high-quality producers would charge, JB says, but they are worth it.

First, the severed legs are pressed, to release as much blood as possible. Next they are salted; they are in salt for a day for every kilo (about 2¼ pounds) of meat, drawing out other liquids. Then they are cleaned and pressed once more, before being hung to dry in the *burja* air, in a closed environment, away from light, away from insects. "Out of the 80 legs I prepare each year, maybe two will not turn out well," he says. A spoiled pršut leg is usually down to a problem in the way the leg was removed from the torso. If there are cracks in the leg bone, bacteria can infiltrate. He then washes the legs periodically with water, dries them, and lets them continue to hang.

When he checks the legs, he uses a primeval tool: the Achilles tendon of a horse. Its tip is honed to a needlepoint, and it looks like a sharp-tipped turkey baster. I immediately want one. No idea what I'd do with it, but I want one.

I love that nothing unnatural enters this process. It's just a pig's leg plus squeezing, salt, squeezing, air, the occasional prod with a horse's tendon, more air, and time. The smell of the inside of the pršut leg, when he draws out the horse tendon probe, tells him all he needs to know about what is happening inside, where along the process he is. "It's the smell," he says. "I can't explain to you what it is I'm smelling. Of course, it can't smell bad, that would indicate a problem. But the way it smells good tells me what more I need." It's a process that requires care, attention to detail, passion. As with any great product.

            Uroš emerges from the kitchen carrying a wooden palette lined with perfectly-rounded, skin-thin curls of pršut. They glisten in the sunshine, held up against the sprawl of the countryside beneath Uroš's farmhouse. Undulations of vineyard rows, white stone houses, sloped hills. I can only imagine what an elaborate dinner here must be like, as Uroš throws a good party (I've been told this, but after five minutes with him this is immediately clear), and he's a master of the grill, too. "The pršut just hangs there and works its magic," he says. "I maybe check on it once a week." The rest of the time he's firing up everything from chops to tripe on a sort of homemade version of a *yakitori* grill that he welded himself, like a long, thin railroad track with a trough in the middle for charcoal. "I realized that the grill itself was a problem. It's a pain to clean it after every service, but if you don't, the blackened bits that stick to it give the next round of meat a burnt taste. So I got rid of the grill and fire my meat on metal skewers, directly over the coals."

A few weeks before visiting Uroš, I finished editing a book by Slovenia's leading food historian, Janez Bogataj, on the tradition of *koline*. This is a term both for the ritual village tradition of slaughtering a pig and also for the many meat products that result from it. Before the dispatching of animals was legally relegated to licensed slaughterhouses, the tradition was that villagers would take turns assisting each other in the slaughter of pigs, one house at a time. Each household would throw a party after the slaughter, to thank the neighbors for their assistance and to share in the porky fruits of their labor. Specialist butchers would move from house to house, leading the *koline*, and taking cuts of meat (and sometimes some money, too) as payment.

There were various, sometimes rather disturbing, rituals associated with this tradition, but one of them was that the youngest children were expected to participate, and one brave youth would be tasked with holding onto the pig's tail during the "main event." It is well-known, and particularly grim, that pigs are perfectly aware of when the bell has tolled for them, and do not go quietly into this dark night. So it is no small task for a seven-year-old to keep hold of a pig's tail, when the pig is in no mood to remain still. Was this a formative trauma, I ask Uroš, knowing that it certainly would be for me. He smiles wide. "I loved it. It was a badge of honor, to hold onto the tail, and it was damn hard to do!"

Uroš once invited fellow pršut producers he admired to a dinner at his farm. One from Spain, bearing *pata negra*, one from Parma. The only rule was that the pršut had to be aged at least two years. He laid his cards on the table, and said his would be aged four years. The judges were the diners that evening. Now that's the sort of dinner party I'd have liked to attend. Can you guess who won?

PROSCIUTTO SLICES
WITH RUTABAGA VARIATIONS

Peel the rutabaga. Cook the peels in salted water, then drain and reserve the water. Dehydrate the peel until very dry and grind into a powder. You can accomplish this by placing on a tray in an oven set to 150°F (65°C) for 4 hours.

Combine the water, sugar, and vinegar. Thin slice some of the rutabaga for chips. Blanch the slices in the water used to cook the peels, then dip them into the sugar water, and put into a dehydrator. Dry the rutabaga slices until crisp to make chips.

Cut four rectangles from the center of the rutabaga (1 x 1 x 3 inches). In a saucepan, prepare a soup from the bones and skin of the prosciutto, simmering them in water for 1.5 hours. Then add the rutabaga rectangles and cook, covered, for 20 minutes. When the rutabaga is cooked, transfer it to another pan, together with the clear soup. (Discard the prosciutto bones and skin.) Leave to cool in the soup.

Cook the remaining rutabaga in the water used to cook the peels until soft, about 25 minutes. Drain and cool. Place half of it into a food processor or Thermomix together with the cottage cheese, season with salt, and blend until smooth. Blend the other half of rutabaga with the sugar syrup, place into a Pacojet beaker or ice cream machine and freeze. Blend the frozen rutabaga in the machine to make rutabaga ice cream. (Alternatively, if an ice cream machine is not available, transfer to a plastic container and freeze. Break or cut into smaller pieces, then blend with an immersion blender until smooth.)

TO SERVE:
Arrange the prosciutto slices (you may cut out circles) on a plate and add the rutabaga chips, cooked rutabaga (discard the soup), the purée, and finally the ice cream.

2 large rutabagas
¼ cup (60 ml) water
2 ounces (60 g) sugar
2½ tablespoons (40 ml) apple cider vinegar
Bones and skin of prosciutto
3 ounces (80 g) cottage cheese
Salt
1½ cups (300 ml) syrup, made from equal parts sugar and water
8 slices prosciutto

PROSCIUTTO-WRAPPED MONKFISH WITH CELERIAC PURÉE, PEACH CREAM, AND OLIVE OIL JELLY

Remove the bone and skin of the monkfish tail, to obtain a fillet.
Arrange the prosciutto on a board, place the monkfish fillet on top, and wrap it in the prosciutto, then wrap in an acetate sheet. Steam for 12 minutes, then remove from the steamer and leave to rest on the board for 4 minutes. Unwrap the parcel and slice. No extra salt is needed, as the prosciutto is salty.

1½ pounds (600 g) monkfish tail
5¼ ounces (150 g) very thin slices prosciutto

CELERIAC:
Peel the celeriac. Cut some very thin slices, preferably with a mandoline, to be used for chips. Cut the remaining celeriac into cubes. Cover the base of a pressure cooker with water and add baking soda and salt. Cook the cubed celeriac for 12 minutes, then transfer to a food processor or Thermomix together with butter and salt. Process to get a smooth purée.

⅔ pound (300 g) celeriac
Pinch of salt and baking soda
3½ ounces (100 g) butter

CHIPS:
Blanch the thin slices of celeriac in salted water for 3 minutes. Drain the slices and place on a silicone mat. Dehydrate in convection oven or in a dehydrator for 2 hours at 160°F (70°C).

OLIVE OIL JELLY:
Pour the water into a saucepan, add the agar agar, and simmer for 10 minutes. Remove from heat and continue stirring. After 5 minutes slowly start adding the olive oil, whisking constantly. Continue whisking until cool. Transfer the cooled mixture into a piping bag.

1 tablespoon (12 g) water
¼ teaspoon (0.7 g) agar agar
1½ tablespoons (25 g) olive oil

PEACH PUREE:
Briefly blanch the peaches, then remove the skins and the pits. Roughly chop the peaches and cook in a saucepan on low heat so that they release some of their juices. Combine the sugar and pectin and add to the peaches. Stir well and cook for 10 minutes. Blend the peaches with an immersion blender to make a smooth purée and fill into a piping bag.

7 ounces (200 g) peaches
3½ tablespoons (50 g) sugar
1½ tablespoons (20 g) pectin

TO SERVE:
First spread the celeriac purée onto a plate with a spatula. Arrange the slices of prosciutto-wrapped monkfish and olive oil jelly on top. Add the peach purée, celeriac chips, and the broccoli sprouts.

Broccoli sprouts

MARJETKA ŽABJEK.
LJUBLJANA CABBAGE.

LJUBLJANA CABBAGE

Sometimes it is the hands that tell the story, other times the smile. Marjetka's father has been a cabbage farmer on the outskirts of Ljubljana his whole life. Their farm is just at the edge of the city, where flat fields stretch out as if reaching for the Alps. His hands are the sort that Renaissance painters would have loved to use as models to show off their technique, for hands and faces have always been considered the most difficult to get right in the world of fine art. His would suit an El Greco, while Marjetka's smile would provide lighting enough for many such paintings. She is luminous and cheerful and joyous and passionate about a very specific thing: Cabbage. More specifically, sauerkraut. According to her family, and anyone you will ask who has been to the Tržnica central market in Ljubljana, her family's sauerkraut is the best in the world. And there's a very specific reason why.

Ljubljana Cabbage is an indigenous type that has been grown here for centuries. It is an endangered species, and as far as Marjetka and her family are aware, there are few other farmers who grow it. At Marjetka's enthusiastic insistence, her father rushes, as quickly as his octogenarian legs allow, back into their home and returns with a linen sack filled with their most valued possession. He reaches those calloused and veined hands deep into the sack and pulls out a handful of seeds that he then allows to cascade between his fingers back into the bag. These are, I am told, the seeds of this special type of cabbage, which the family cultivates and preserves for years, decades, and even though the seeds with the same name can be bought in seed stores as well, Marjetka says they are quite different.

Perhaps it is the way in which the family talks about and handles this precious cargo, treating it as if it were some miraculous ancient relic, or maybe something about the way that Marjetka says the word "cabbage" (punching out the consonants with her lips), in her lovely accented English, that gives you a sense that this is the good stuff. It is one of several varieties that her family grows, along with a myriad of other vegetables, but this is their claim to fame, the reason why they are the ones with the long lines every day at the central market.

They plant the seeds at many different locations, not only at their farm on the outskirts of the capital, but also on another plot of land in the marshy region on the far side of the city, the soil of which has a constant supply of moisture and nutrients to feed the cabbage, even when the temperatures and fickle weather do not permit it to thrive just a couple miles away, on the other side of town. They have also experimented with planting seeds in all manner of different terrain around Slovenia, with some fields higher up in the mountains, some in drier, rockier areas. Though they would never classify themselves as such, they are informal scientists.

Sauerkraut is an ancient staple vegetable, as cabbage is ubiquitous and thrives and is easy to grow and inexpensive. Fermenting it is the ancient trick that makes it so valuable. When allowed to sit in salt, it transforms into something that can last a very long time indeed, preserved and morphed and fermented and absolutely lovely. Nothing goes into Marjetka's sauerkraut except for this unique type of cabbage, salt, and time. During the summer, the fresh cabbage is transformed into sauerkraut in just three weeks, whereas it takes two months during the winter.

Sauerkraut is associated with the food of hearty mountain peasants and workers. And there is something to it. Sauerkraut is filling and nutritious and provides plenty of vitamins and energy to keep you going in winter months. It is the perfect accompaniment to a saucy chop or sausage, and that is how Slovenians normally eat it, as well. But these methods can be refined, as they are in the hands of JB.

"For me, sauerkraut is best with bratwurst, sour turnip with blood sausage," he says. "For sauerkraut, I eat it raw as soon as I've bought it. If it's too bitter, I boil it in water for ten to fifteen minutes. Then I pour out half the water and replace it with fresh water. In a pan, I'll fry some *ocvirki* (pork cracklings) and a tiny bit of flour. Then I take the sauerkraut out of the water and put it into the pan, spooning in just a little water at a time. For sour turnip, I try to make it juicier. I dry the *ocvirki* then add them to the boiled turnip, along with a little flour."

Slovenians also enjoy red cabbage, particularly on the feast of Saint Martin's Day (November 11), when new wine is poured and the traditional meal is a centerpiece of roasted goose or duck, sided by *mlinci*, similar to tortillas, and red cabbage. Something that was entirely new to me was Slovenian sour turnip, *kisla repa*, which tastes a lot better than it sounds. It is turnip, sliced into strips and prepared just as you would prepare sauerkraut. It is exquisite, with a similar taste to sauerkraut but a rather different texture. Pepped up with *ocvirki*, and in a pool of that beautiful, white and (relatively) healthful pork lard, it is as sophisticated in flavor as you could hope for, and as simple. These are the sort of foods that farmers could make when their crops were fresh and then preserve for those rough winter months, ideal to offset precious cuts of meat and soak up the juices–a huge mound of sauerkraut makes a small portion of meat feel generous.

We in the West tend to associate fermentation with an arcane art of the Far East, with Korea being a particular mecca for it, but the process of fermentation as a preservative and flavor booster has always been alive and well in Europe, though normally in the less-refined cuisines. I am always more interested in, and more appetized by, what so-called "peasants" used to eat, than the airy delicacies of the aristocracy. I'll take a giant pile of sauerkraut over anything more fancy-pants, any day.

There are medicinal benefits to it, too, as Marjetka is happy to announce. One day at her stand at the market, I couldn't help but notice some oddly homemade-looking water bottles that had been converted into something that advertised itself as "sauerkraut juice." That sounded like some sort of line from *The Simpsons*, but when I asked Marjetka about it, she assured me that not only does it taste better than you'd think it would, but that doctors recommend it to patients as a home cure for two distinct ailments. If you have trouble in the, um, bathroom department, drinking some of this will soon end your sorrows and "release the valve," so to speak. And if you had too much alcohol the night before, then drinking this the next morning will quickly end your hangover. Delicious and medicinal? Sign me up.

There could be no more traditional Slovenian dish than a plate of Marjetka's Ljubljana cabbage, transmuted into sauerkraut, with sausages. What might be mistaken for a grandmother's inexpensive Sunday winter luncheon, with frost cracking the ground outside and dusting the windows with its breath, and the heat of a tiled stove emanating within, to warm the slippered feet of the extended family gathered around, when cooked up in JB's hands is elevated to a refined art form. But it all starts with the best of ingredients and, from personal experience and from all I've heard others say, there is no better sauerkraut than that produced by Marjetka and her family, from an endangered linen sack full of very special seeds.

ROAST SUCKLING PIG WITH SAUERKRAUT AND CRACKLINGS, AND BUTTER-BAKED JACKET POTATOES WITH SOUR CREAM

Season the whole loin rack with salt and rub with crushed garlic. Place in a saucepan and add just enough water to cover the base of the pan. Add the vegetables and herbs and cook, covered, on low heat for 45 minutes.
Heat the oven to 350°F (175°C).
Transfer the meat to a baking tray, add the juices from the saucepan to the tray, together with the vegetables, and roast in the oven about 25 minutes. Baste the meat frequently with the roasting juices, ensuring that the skin becomes golden brown and crisp. Towards the end, the oven fan may be turned on for a few minutes.

2¼ pounds (1 kg) loin rack from Krško polje (Blackstrap) suckling
1 ounce (30 g) salt
3 cloves garlic, crushed
1 sprig thyme
1 onion
½ celeriac
1 carrot
2 bay leaves

SOUR TURNIP:
Taste the sour turnip and rinse if it is too sour. Place into a pot and bring to a boil, then drain the water, add fresh water, season with salt and bay leaf, and cook for 45 minutes. Drain approximately half the water.
In a small bowl, whisk the flour and cold water and add to the turnip. Cook a further 10 minutes, then remove the bay leaf.

1½ pounds (600 g) sour turnip
Salt
1 bay leaf
2 ounces (60 g) flour
½ cup (100 ml) cold water

POTATOES:
Scrub the potatoes well and cook them in salted water for 25 minutes, then remove from the water and fry in clarified butter.
Combine the sour cream and softened butter and mix well. When the potatoes are fried, gently press them so that they split open. Spoon the sour cream and butter mixture into the opening and sprinkle with snipped chives.

4 small potatoes
2 ounces (60 g) clarified butter (ghee)
5½ ounces (160 g) sour cream
1¾ ounces (50 g) softened butter
Salt
Chives

TO SERVE:
Slice the meat into cutlets. Briefly fry the cracklings and sprinkle them onto the sour turnip, then add this to the meat. Pour some roasting juices over the top and place a potato on each plate.

5¼ ounces (150 g) Krško polje (Blackstrap) pork cracklings

SAUERKRAUT SORBET

Soak the gelatin in cold water to soften.

Bring the sauerkraut juice, glucose syrup, and sugar to a boil. Squeeze out the excess water from the gelatin and add to the syrup. Stir in the sauerkraut and blend with an immersion blender, then transfer to a Pacojet beaker or ice cream machine and freeze for 24 hours.

TO SERVE:
Remove the sorbet from the freezer and blend in the machine. If an ice cream machine is not available, place the sorbet in a plastic container and freeze. Break or cut the sorbet into smaller pieces, then blend with an immersion blender until smooth.

Remove the central vein from the whole sauerkraut leaves and halve the leaves. Place a half leaf on the bottom of a bowl and top with a scoop of sorbet.

2 teaspoons gelatin powder (6 g gelatin leaves)
4½ ounces (130 g) sauerkraut juice
1 ounce (30 g) glucose syrup
1¾ ounces (50 g) sugar
1 pound + 2 ounces (500 g) sauerkraut
2 whole sauerkraut leaves

DR. KATJA REBOLJ
AND PETER ZAJC, ROŽMA.
WILD HERBS AND FLOWERS.

WILD HERBS AND FLOWERS

His name, believe it or not, is Peter Rabbit. That's the direct translation of Peter Zajc. If it were not adorable enough that his name is Peter Rabbit, he has many qualities, among which is being quite adorable. The Latin phrase *nomen est omen* comes to mind. Together with his business partner, Dr. Katja Rebolj, they are among the leading herb hunters in Slovenia, setting out on commission for the country's top chefs. The two of them, longtime friends, decided to combine their hobby and passion with a profession.

We meet them in a lovely suburban garden behind a ramshackle farmhouse not far from the main road that leads to Ljubljana. The town of Trzin is just fifteen minutes from the capital but feels very rural. It is also where JB grew up, in a house that is no longer, but was once just a few hundred yards from where we now stand. Katja is wandering barefoot, as she likes to feel the growths beneath her feet and grass between her toes. She and Peter talk eagerly about this herb garden and the wild fringes of a grass meadow, while JB bends over and picks up what looks to me like grass, or perhaps a weed. To me, it's something in need of mowing. For him, it looks like lunch. He has a habit of feeding me things torn from the ground that I would wholly ignore, much less consider a potential ingredient. This is slightly weird at first, but then great fun. The world is his cupboard. But you need to know what's good and what's good for you. A Slovenian favorite, *čemaž*, ramson or wild garlic, has broad, green leaves that look a bit too much like another grass that will kill you. In fact, there are fatalities almost every year from people who thought they were gathering wild garlic for lunch and wound up with *jesenski podlesek* (*Colchicum autumnale*) instead, a plant which causes arsenic-like poison symptoms and for which there is no known cure. But wild garlic, perhaps like *fugu*, the delicious bit of the blowfish that happens to be near the toxic bit, is worth the risk. Pungent and intensely green, like the strongest garlic you could imagine, it must be used in sensible quantities. I once made the mistake of thinking that a jar labelled "*čemaž pesto*" was to be used like a jar of normal pesto, just poured over cooked pasta. It tasted so garlic-tastic that my eyes started to water. The apartment was garlic-scented for days thereafter, and my wife forbade the use of *čemaž* in closed spaces. It's delicious and, well, potent.

These vast fields of wild alpine grasses and flowers, so picturesque, that stretch throughout the northern region of Slovenia, are mainly edible, imparting nutrients and vitamins galore. It is impossible to go hungry, if you know what you're looking for here in the Alps. You have fresh salad available in every field. Peter remembers growing up and eagerly foraging for wild herbs with his parents, a special bonding time for them, the way some children might play ball or go for a hike or watch movies. He would take to the woods and fields to gather, as humans and animals have for as long as they have existed. There is a beauty in continuing that tradition. It is part of a continuum of what it is to be human. It requires no wallet, no gun, nothing but knowledge and the will to seek out natural treasures.

Some of them really do require searching. Katja and Peter have gotten to the point where they now take specific orders from restaurants, essentially foraging on commission. They have an encyclopedic knowledge of floral life here in the Alps, with university degrees to back up what they have learned in the field and from the mouths of family members, of grandmothers with gnarled knuckles and mountain wisdom. I am grateful for people like Peter and Katja, who preserve such knowledge and combine it with the latest scientific research. It is an ideal combination.

The two will make the rounds of high-end restaurants and catering services and the occasional private customer, first offering a steady array of what has been freshly gathered. But they will also set off on particular expeditions, some of which take them high into the mountains, require hours of hiking, and which are by no means a stroll in a field. Many of the plants they gather have medicinal properties, as well as gastronomic ones. I can attest to the sinus-cleansing powers of *čemaž* and *hren*, horseradish, for instance.

They take us around the garden and point out various plants, mentioning which parts of them are used and with which preparations, but also what they do for the human body. For instance, *zajčja deteljica*, wood sorrel (*Oxalis acetosella*), found in the forests, has a vinegar-y taste. Tolščak, common purslane (*Portulaca oleracea*), is packed with omega-3 fatty acids, and is beneficial for folks with lipid issues, a good substitute for fish oil. Kapucinka, garden nasturtium (*Tropaeolum majus*), a beautiful butter-yellow flower, has a powerful taste that JB likes to use to offset a good steak or corn soup. *Trpotec*, plantago, is nicknamed "vegetarian cracklings," as it tastes like pork skin, when fried. *Črna detelja*, red clover (*Trifolium pratense*), is often used to decorate plates, but is also a great source of calcium, iron, and riboflavin (vitamin B2). *Kislica*, sorrel (*Rumex acetosa*), has a pleasant sour taste, and while most chefs would use only the stalks, JB likes to prepare the roots. He is like a kid in a candy store, but the candy here is free—you just have to know what to pick, and how to integrate it.

It is fascinating to see how JB transforms this information into recipes. For instance, he invented a wild flora mayonnaise made of dandelion greens, plantago, and various meadow grasses, placed into a blender and blended with a stream of Lisjak olive oil, then sieved. The result is a green, raw food, an entirely healthy and delicious "mayonnaise."

He gathers the wisdom of these two gatherers the way they gather plants. He harnesses the information and, when he bites into what looks like a blade of grass, his sense of taste translates this sensory information, in his mind, into recipe possibilities. Perhaps like a great painter, who might encounter a new pigment and, without testing it, be able to imagine how to integrate it into their works, and then do so seamlessly. I guess I have something similar, but in a less practical vein. I hear an interesting idea or meet an interesting character, and I automatically transform them into a potential article or section of a book.

But what I do you can't eat. I prefer JB's version. And I'll let him make the čemaž at his place. Some things are better eaten than smelled in enclosed spaces.

RUNNER BEANS WITH PURSLANE AND WILD GARLIC BULBS, CHERRY TOMATOES, AND PARSNIP FOAM

Trim the runner beans and cook in salted water for 20 minutes or until tender.

14 ounces (400 g) runner beans

Blanch and peel the tomatoes.

8 cherry tomatoes

Peel the parsnip, cut into small pieces, and place into a pressure cooker with a little water and baking soda. Cook for 10 minutes. Blend the cooked parsnip with ¼ cup (50 ml) olive oil to make a cream. Transfer the cream into a whipping siphon.

¼ pound (120 g) parsnip
½ cup (100 ml) olive oil, divided

Blanch the wild garlic bulbs for 1 minute.

12 bulbs wild garlic (ramsons)

Heat the remaining olive oil in a pan and add the beans, purslane, tomatoes, and wild garlic. Fry quickly and season with more salt if necessary.

4¼ ounces (120 g) purslane
Salt, pepper, baking soda

TO SERVE:
Arrange the runner beans on a plate, then the tomatoes, wild garlic, and purslane. Spread the parsnip foam over the top.

GARDEN SNAILS BAKED
IN LARDO WITH WILD HERBS

Cook the fresh snails in their shells in salted water for an hour and a half together with the vegetables. Slice the garlic as thin as possible and arrange it on the lardo slices. Remove the cooked snails from their shells and clean them, removing the innards, then wrap in the slices of lardo.

12 snails in shells
Vegetables: 1 carrot, a piece of celeriac, a piece of leek, a piece of rutabaga, ½ onion, 1 parsley root
1 clove garlic
12 thin slices lardo
Salt

Cook the tapioca in salted water for 15 minutes, remove from the heat, and set aside for 5 minutes, then drain and rinse well under cold running water.

4¼ ounces (120 g) tapioca pearls
Salt
4¼ cups (1 L) water

Blanch the spinach and herbs for 3 minutes, then place into iced water to cool quickly. Drain and blend in a food processor or Thermomix until smooth. Spread some of the herb cream on a silicone mat and dry in a dehydrator, then grind in a coffee grinder to a powder. Put some of the cream into a piping bag.

1¾ ounces (50 g) spinach
1 ounce (30 g) lovage
⅔ ounce (20 g) narrowleaf plantain
⅔ ounce (20 g) yarrow
1 ounce (30 g) dandelion leaves
⅔ ounce (20 g) maidenstears
1½ ounces (40 g) butter
Salt

Heat the remaining herb cream in a saucepan, add the tapioca, butter, and salt and cook for 5 minutes.

Carefully fry the snails on all sides.

TO SERVE:
Spoon the tapioca with herbs into a bowl, sprinkle with the herb powder and pipe dots of the herb purée. Arrange the fried snails on top.

GORAZD TRUŠNOVEC,
URBAN BEEKEEPER.
CARNIOLAN GRAY BEE
POLLEN AND HONEY.

CARNIOLAN GRAY BEE POLLEN AND HONEY

Gorazd Trušnovec, when he was in his mid-thirties, suddenly missed the smell of beehives. In Slovenia, this Proustian moment might not sound quite so odd as it likely does in other contexts. Slovenia has an inordinate number of beekeepers per capita—the most in the world, in fact. It is a very rich tradition and one that is deeply rooted in the culture. Still, for a young man living in the heart of the capital, trained as an architect and having edited Slovenia's premiere film magazine, it was a return to folk roots that he had not known he had.

Slovenia boasts five beekeepers per thousand people, making it a hobby more common here than playing chess. Its ubiquity gave birth to an indigenous art form, painted bee hive panels, which are illustrated with charming and funny scenes of religious motifs or folk sayings, like a commentary on the sharp tongue of old women in a village, with an image of a gossip having her tongue sharpened on a sharpening stone, or world-turned-upside-down images of animals hunting hunters.

Most of the beekeeping in Slovenia is just for home use, a hive or two to produce enough honey for home consumption and as a gift for friends. Slovenia was slow to shift to urban beekeeping which, in recent years, has grown so popular abroad that, in London, most apartment buildings seem to have hives on the roof. This sounds good at first, but in London there is not enough greenery to feed the multitude of bees kept there, and so the bees are in danger of starving. Not so in Ljubljana, a very green capital. In fact, it was named "green capital of Europe" in 2016 and it is packed with parks and trees. This is where Gorazd set up the first urban beekeeping society in Slovenia.

At first, he was looked upon with mirth and confusion by the locals. Beekeeping, yes, but in the middle of the capital city? That Proustian moment, Gorazd only realized much later, recalled fond memories of his youth when his uncle, who kept bees rurally, would bring his mobile beehives to a field behind Gorazd's grandmother's house, which was full of acacia blossoms. That combined scent of honey and insect life and pollen and linseed oil–covered wood and the outdoors was a powerful cocktail for young Gorazd.

It was this scent that returned to him in his thirties. It felt odd to him, because he was a city guy who had never given a second thought to bees since his childhood. But the call was upon him, so he began to study. For about a year, he read everything he could about beekeeping, buying books and scouring the internet for any lesson he could gather. He also met the godfather of urban beekeeping in Ljubljana, Franc Petrovčiča, who had set up the very first urban hives in the country, atop the national cultural center, Cankarjev dom, in the center of the city. He offered himself as an apprentice to Petrovčiča and learned as much as he could. He also found out the hard way that the process of learning to be a beekeeper is slow and sometimes painful. He has been stung innumerable times, and while some macho beekeepers say they don't even feel it, he jokes, a sting is a sting and it is no fun. It also hurts the hive, because 90 percent of bees that sting in self-defense die because their stinger tears off of their bodies when they try to flee after the attack.

Bees function in a semi-dictatorial society, or perhaps a parliamentary dictatorship. The queen governs the rhythm of the hive and can lay over 2,000 eggs in a single day. But if she is not doing her job well, the bees can overthrow her and replace her with someone else. In order to start a new hive, you have to get a queen bee to shift to new digs. When hives get too full, bees have an instinct that half of the population should leave and start a new hive. The first place they look for a new spot to set up shop is within a few meters of the old hive. If this sounds a bit like teenagers moving out of the house, then there may be something to that. Bees, like teens, raid the pantry for three days' worth of food and then scoot, and if you happen to set up a suitable hive space adjacent to the previous one at the right time, then they might move into your new hive. This is how hives multiply and farmers can share their bee families with others looking to acquire them.

Bees are not particular fans of the winter and there can be as few as 9,000 in one of Gorazd's hives, which he describes as the lowest number that still maintains its functionality. But come May, there can be as many as 40,000 in a single hive, which is when it may be time to make like a stock and split.

The only type of bee that is permitted in Slovenia is the indigenous Carniolan honey bee, also known as gray bee. This type of bee is the second most-sought-after in the world, as it is particularly well-suited to temperate climates with varying seasonal weather patterns and it is extremely docile, thus easy to work with (think minimal stings). In order to keep the indigenous bloodline clean, it is illegal to keep other types of honey bees here. I joke with Gorazd that this sounds a bit like far-right-wing politics, but when it comes to maintaining a potentially endangered animal species, I suppose it is not so objectionable.

The Carniolan gray bees are indeed a gray color and are indeed very calm. When Gorazd opens one of his hives, housing one of the fifty families of bees that he keeps at fifteen different locations around the capital, he pumps smoke around and wears gloves at first. But then he sees that they are so relaxed that he no longer needs the smoke and he takes his gloves off to work. Neither he nor I are even approached by a bee, much less stung. I wore one of those netted beekeeper hats, but mostly because I thought it was really cool, not for defensive purposes.

> The smoke that beekeepers use can be of any type, and Gorazd just burns a little scrap of cellulose salvaged from the recycling bin. The smoke does not make the bees drowsy, as I had mistakenly imagined, but in fact triggers their fire alarm instinct. Gorazd explains that bees have no natural defense against fires, but intuitively they gather three days' worth of honey to provide sustenance and flee the hive. If a real fire were present, then they would pick up and create a new hive somewhere else, living off these supplies until the new hive was ready. So, the smoke triggers this reaction and the bees launch into panic mode. It takes them ten to fifteen minutes to figure out that there isn't actually a fire and that you, the beekeeper, are the problem. Then, as Gorazd jokes, they get really pissed off. At that point, it's best for the beekeeper to cease operations and go grab a beer, otherwise he will incur the wrath of the hive.

This is why beginner beekeepers can run into problems. Once you open a hive, you only have around ten minutes to do whatever it is you need to do that day. After that the bees get annoyed with you and consider you an intruder. Gorazd is careful to underscore that bees are not pets. And they are not mammals, with that attachment instinct of companionship that mammals possess. They are insects and have millions of years of programmed instincts running through them. They do not like you as a beekeeper. They consider you a thief trying to take their honey, which in actuality is just what you are. But knowing that, you can take some precautionary measures. The smoke is a useful one, but it provides you with only a little bit of time. You should only engage in beekeeping if you are relaxed and in a good mood, as Gorazd explains that bees can sense foul states of mind. They are especially sensitive to adrenaline, and they associate it with an attack. If you are relaxed enough then the bees will be relaxed, too. If you move slowly enough, they do not associate such movement with intrusion and will go about their business, ignoring you.

When JB had told me that he wanted us to visit an urban beekeeper, I naively assumed that the featured ingredient of this chapter would be honey. *Au contraire.* What JB orders from Gorazd is not only honey but mostly pollen. There are several products that humans can benefit from harvesting from their kept bees, and honey is just one of them. Pollen is actually what the bees themselves eat. They eat honey only occasionally, when they need a burst of extra energy, but pollen is their daily bread. Gorazd explains that pollen contains everything that an organism needs to live indefinitely, including an ideal balance of protein and vitamins and carbohydrates and fats. A human could live indefinitely off of pollen, if necessary and if enough of it were made available. When bees go out into the world, they gather up pollen, which sticks in yellow clumps to their hind legs. When Gorazd wants to collect pollen, he attaches a special membrane to the front of the hive that the bees have to squeeze through, in order to return home. This membrane scratches off and captures about 30 percent of the pollen that the bee brought back with him. What follows is a fairly comical interlude. The bee pushes through the membrane, looks back and sees that he has less pollen gathered about his hind legs than he'd thought, and scoots back out into the world to gather more. That pollen can be gathered in amounts of up to several kilos (about 2¼ pounds) per a hive. It has a very subtle but distinct honey-like taste that JB loves to integrate as a surprise grace note to his dishes.

I've seen different types of honey sold—acacia, chestnut, forest—but I never knew just what the difference was, even thinking that it was produced by different types of bees (what I do not know could fill a library). Gorazd tells me that the different types refer to the type of tree prevalent in forests where mobile hives can be set up for periods of a few weeks at a time, when bees feed off of the local trees nearest to where their hive has been carried. When chestnut trees are in bloom, and bees are brought to the chestnuts, they will gather this pollen and produce chestnut honey, and so on. When Gorazd's uncle drove his mobile hives to his grandmother's country house, he did so to produce acacia honey, as those trees prevailed there. Gorazd himself was surprised to learn, when he first began his urban beekeeping, that the honey his Ljubljana-based bees produced, in the center of a substantial city, was categorized as "forest honey" (from pollen gathered from a mixture of trees). This is explained by the numerous, large parks that lie within or just on the edge of wonderfully-lush Ljubljana. The bees can fly a long way, three to five kilometers (up to three miles), to get what they need. They have no trouble flying such distances nor flying up to the top of skyscrapers. They also gather more pollen from a tree than from fields of flowers. In fact, one tree gives them the equivalent pollen of 100 square meters (more than 1,000 square feet) of fields or flowers. So, they are truly forest creatures, and have developed over millions of years as such.

Humans have been part of this loop of blossom to pollen to bee to honey for millennia, and it is a symbiotic relationship. And since Slovenia is truly the land of beekeepers, this is the place to sample the pollen that is, and is directly from, the bee's knees.

YOGURT PANNA COTTA WITH MANDARIN SORBET, WHITE CHOCOLATE SPONGE CAKE, AND HONEY SAUCE

PANNA COTTA:

Soak the gelatin in cold water to soften. Bring the cream and sugar to a boil and add the gelatin, squeezed of excess water. Combine the cream mixture with the yogurt and pour into four small silicone molds. Leave in the freezer overnight. If an ice cream machine is not available, place the sorbet in a plastic container and freeze. Break or cut the sorbet into smaller pieces, then blend with an immersion blender until smooth.

4 teaspoons gelatin powder (4 leaves gelatin)
6 ounces (168 g) whipping cream
3 ounces (84 g) sugar
10 ounces (285 g) plain yogurt

SORBET:

Soak the gelatin in cold water to soften. Bring the sugar, glucose, and water to a boil and add the squeezed-out gelatin. Combine the mandarin and lemon juices and add to the sugar syrup. Pour into a Pacojet beaker or ice cream machine and freeze. If an ice cream machine is not available, place the sorbet in a plastic container and freeze. Break or cut the sorbet into smaller pieces, then blend with an immersion blender until smooth.

2 teaspoons gelatin powder (6 g gelatin leaves)
⅓ cup (90 g) sugar
1 ounce (30 g) glucose syrup
4¼ ounces (122 g) water
2 cups (500 g) mandarin juice
1 tablespoon (10 g) lemon juice

SPONGE CAKES:

Melt the chocolate in a double boiler. Add the eggs and yolk, sugar, and flour and whisk until well combined. Pour into a whipping siphon, add two chargers, and put in the fridge for an hour. Then pipe the batter into four plastic or paper cups and microwave for 1 minute on medium power. When the cakes are baked, leave to cool, then remove from the cups and break into pieces before serving.

⅔ ounce (20 g) white chocolate
2 eggs
1 egg yolk
½ ounce (15 g) sugar
1 ounce (30 g) all-purpose flour

HONEY SAUCE:

Soak the gelatin in cold water to soften. Heat the honey and cream on low. When the honey melts, remove from the stove, add the squeezed out gelatin, and whisk until the sauce has cooled and is smooth.

1 heaping teaspoon gelatin powder (4 g gelatin leaves)
3½ tablespoons (50 g) honey
½ cup (100 ml) whipping cream

JELLY:

Boil the mandarin juice, sugar, and agar agar, then cool and blend to a smooth jelly.

1¾ cups (380 g) mandarin juice
1½ tablespoons (20 g) sugar
2 teaspoons (5 g) agar agar

TO SERVE:

Turn the molds upside down on plates to release the panna cottas. Add the honey sauce, jelly, crumbled cakes, and sorbet.

FRIED AND COOKED BEEF TENDONS WITH HONEY IN WILD GARLIC SAUCE, WITH COLD-PRESSED SUNFLOWER OIL, VINEGAR, AND WILD HERBS

Soak the tendons overnight in cold water. The next day, transfer to a pot, cover with water, add the vegetables and spices, and simmer, covered, for 5 to 6 hours, until the tendons are tender. Remove the cooked tendons from the liquid (reserve the liquid), clean, removing the mushy layer, leave to cool, and cut into small pieces. Pour the honey into a saucepan together with ¼ cup (50 ml) of the cooking liquid, add half of the tendon pieces, and heat through. Coat the remaining tendon pieces first in flour, then through beaten egg and breadcrumbs, then deep-fry in oil.

2¼ pounds (1 kg) beef tendons
1 carrot
1 onion
2 cloves garlic
1 bay leaf
Black pepper
1 tablespoon silver fir honey
3½ tablespoons (50 g) flour
1 egg
3½ tablespoons (50 g) breadcrumbs
1½ cups (300 ml) oil for deep-frying

WILD GARLIC PURÉE:
Wash the wild garlic and spinach and steam for 5 minutes, then immediately transfer to iced water to cool.
Drain the wild garlic and spinach and transfer to a saucepan, adding some of the liquid in which the tendons were cooked if needed. Heat through, season with salt and pepper, and process to a smooth purée.

10½ ounces (300 g) wild garlic leaves (ramsons)
5¼ ounces (150 g) spinach
Salt and pepper

TO SERVE:
Pour the wild garlic purée onto a plate, place the honeyed and the deep-fried tendon pieces on top, drizzle with cold-pressed sunflower oil, scatter wild herbs, and serve with a few drops of wine vinegar.

¼ cup (50 ml) cold-pressed sunflower oil
Wild herbs to decorate
Wine vinegar

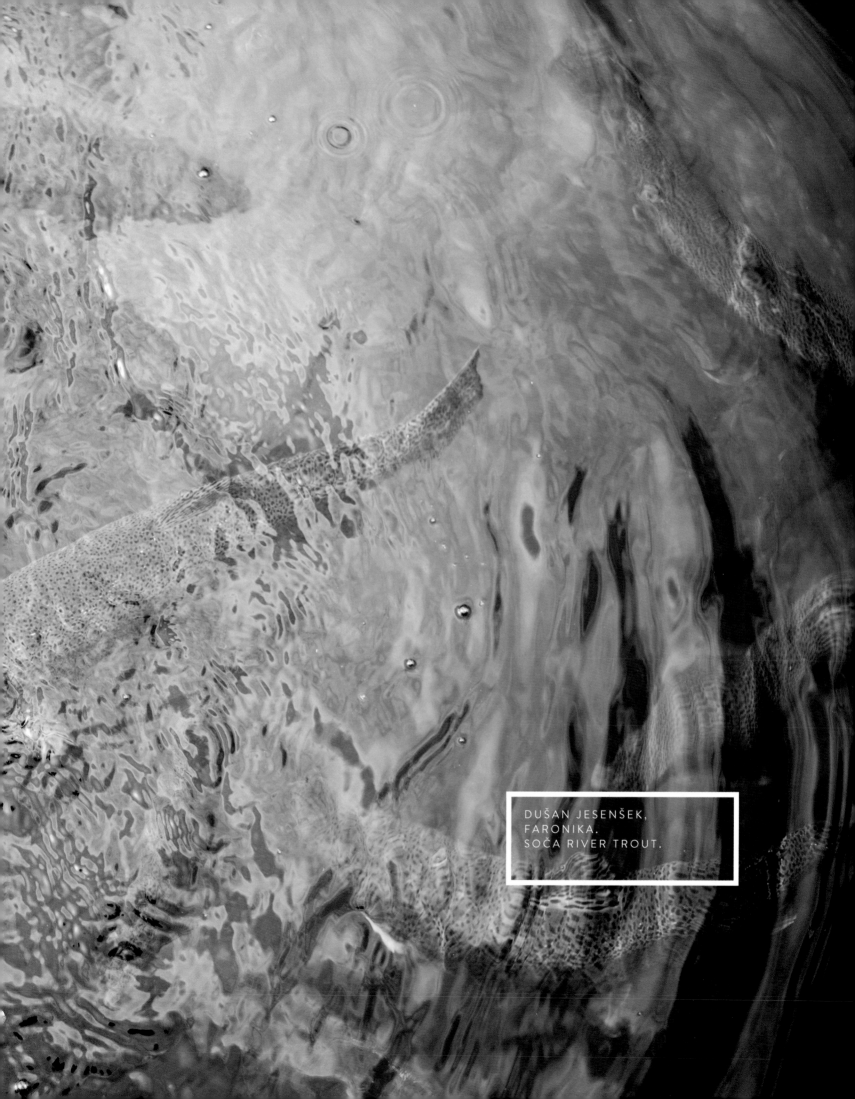

DUŠAN JESENŠEK,
FARONIKA.
SOČA RIVER TROUT.

SOČA RIVER TROUT

First, let it be said that they are huge. Monster trouts, twice the size of their more common cousins, and with a gorgeous, mottled leopard-spot design on their scales. Due to a single piece of technology put to improper use they very nearly went extinct over just a two-year period. From 1915–1917, the Soča (Isonzo) Front, a territory along the Italy/Slovenia border near the Soča River, was the scene of some of the most casualty-heavy fighting of the First World War, with more than a million people killed, wounded, vanished, and captured there in just two years. The setting for Ernest Hemingway's *A Farewell to Arms*, the Soča River is also a place of immense natural beauty, named by the *Huffington Post* as "the most beautiful river in the world." During the war, hungry soldiers resorted to whatever measures they could to gather up a meal. Fishing took time and left you open to the enemy. It was far faster, and more efficient, to "fish" with grenades. Soldiers would lob bombs into the Soča River. When they blew up, they killed everything beneath the emerald water, and scores of fish would float to the surface, to be retrieved and eaten. It was far too efficient. This method, in this narrow period, almost completely wiped out a species of trout that only exists in this one river and its tributaries, in the mountains of Slovenia. Cross-breeding didn't help, either.

Sometimes called a "marble trout," this is one of the largest in the trout family, with a world-record fish having weighed in at an astounding 55.1 pounds. It is also considered the most subtle and delicious of the species, and indeed among all freshwater fish, worldwide.

To rescue this remarkable species and bring it back from the edge of extinction, while still allowing a selection of top chefs to serve it at their restaurants, a team set up the Faronika Fish Farm in Tolmin, not far from the restaurant that is best-known for serving Soča River Trout, Hiša Franko, run by the 2017 World's Best Female Chef, Ana Roš, a friend and colleague of JB. Opened in 2016, Faronika Fish Farm has the capacity to raise 40 to 45 tons of trout per year, most of which are more common varieties (with 35 tons of rainbow trout), but they still hope to raise some 3 to 4 tons of Soča river trout per annum–and the fish often weigh around 20 kilos each (about 45 pounds).

According to Dušan Jesenšek, a marine biologist specializing in Soča river trout and director of the Faronika Fish Farm, the fish are slow to grow. "As a result of this slow growth, their flesh has a particular texture and flavor that is different from fish who have a more intense and rapid growth period. The flesh is more subtle and easier to digest, and so is often served raw, as *carpaccio*, to experience the full flavor." Dušan and his colleagues were able to bring back the Soča river trout from the brink of extinction because their DNA was similar enough to other breeds of sea trout (for Soča river trout can live in salt or fresh water) that they could be cross-bred. While there are now Soča river trouts in the wild, their populations can vary dramatically. In one of the tributaries of the Soča, Dušan said that his team counted 270 fish during one round of monitoring. But just a few weeks later, with reduced rainfall, it was down to 12.

Tolmin and its surrounding towns in the Julian Alps, like Bovec and Kobarid, are not so far off the beaten track when you look at a map, but they are difficult to reach from the rest of Slovenia. To date, there are only local, very windy roads, and it is actually faster to drive to Italy on the highway and access these border towns from the Italian side. Kobarid has an award-winning museum of the First World War, and the *Narnia* films had scenes shot here, as the terrain looks suitably for some fantasy realm, particularly the almost artificial-looking turquoise of the Soča River. It is a place that feels far-flung, but that is part of its charm. You wouldn't stumble upon it but must make a pilgrimage. And its pilgrims are rewarded.

Thanks to the efforts of folks like Dušan, the Soča river trout is no longer officially an endangered species, but as he says, "It doesn't mean that we can relax." Responsible sport fishermen always catch and release Soča river trout (after taking a selfie), which means that the only such trout you can eat come from Faronika Fish Farm. At least, that's what's supposed to happen. There's a danger in being so wildly delicious.

COLD-SMOKED SOČA TROUT WITH SAUCE, MANDARIN MARMALADE, TROUT ROE, AND DAIKON RADISH

Fillet the trout and remove all bones. Place the head and bones in cold water. Add the kombu kelp and cook on medium heat for 10 minutes, then strain and add salt and soy sauce.

3¼ pounds (1.5 kg) whole cold-smoked trout
1½ cups (300 ml) cold water
1 sheet kombu kelp
¼ cup (50 ml) low-sodium soy sauce
Salt

DAIKON:

Thin slice the daikon. Measure ½ cup (100 ml) fish stock, combine with white vinegar, add daikon slices, and cook for 5 minutes. Leave to cool and marinate overnight.

3½ ounces (100 g) daikon
2 tablespoons (30 ml) white vinegar

Place the fish skin in the canola oil and heat to approximately 175°F (80°C), then leave overnight to enhance the flavors.

½ cup (100 ml) canola oil for fish skin

MANDARIN MARMALADE:

Prepare the marmalade on the same day as the fish. Cook whole unpeeled mandarins in water for 35 minutes. Remove from the water, leave to cool, halve, and remove seeds. Chop the halves, including the rinds, into small pieces, place into a saucepan, and add the combined sugar and pectin. Cook for half an hour, then mash to make a smooth marmalade. Leave to cool overnight.

6 organic mandarins
½ cup (100 g) sugar
3½ tablespoons (50 g) pectin

Place the remaining stock (1¼ cups, or 250 ml) in a container and blend with an immersion blender, gradually adding ½ cup (100 ml) olive oil, to obtain an emulsion.

½ cup (100 ml) olive oil

TO SERVE:

Slice the trout as thin as possible and arrange in a bowl, forming a wreath. Pour the emulsion into the center and decorate with drops of the canola oil. Decorate with trout roe, wholegrain mustard, mandarin marmalade, cooked lentils, marinated daikon, and chervil.

Trout roe
Wholegrain mustard
3½ tablespoons (50 g) cooked black lentils
Chervil for decoration

BLUE-COOKED SOČA TROUT WITH VINEGAR AND VEGETABLES

Gut the trout and remove the gills. Don't rinse the fish too much, as the mucus must remain on the fish to give it its distinctive blue color.

Choose a large pot to fit the fish, preferably a fish poacher. First place the vegetables and salt in the pot with 6½ cups (1.5 L) water and vinegar and cook on low heat for 10 minutes, then add the fish and herbs. The water should just cover the fish. Remove from heat and leave, covered, for 20 minutes. Return the pot to the stove, just long enough for the soup to heat up.
When the fish is cooked, serve with soup and vegetables.

3¼ pounds (1.5 kg) trout

1 carrot
1 rutabaga
1 Jerusalem artichoke
1 stalk celery
Salt
6½ cups (1.5 L) water
¼ cup (50 ml) vinegar
1 sprig rosemary
2 sage leaves

MIRAN IVANETIČ.
BEEF.

BEEF

———————

Miran Ivanetič can tell, from the moment he sees a client approaching his butcher shop in the remote southern Slovenian town of Črnomelj, what that client is going to order. The majority of his regulars are men, and something about the way they approach gives it away. This is a lively place, particularly on a Saturday morning. A visit to the local butcher, a chat, and perhaps even a friendly glass of wine while they wait is one of the week's small delights. Some come in for steak, some for burgers, some for čevapčiči (the "burger of the Balkans," an oblong grilled meatball served just about anywhere you go in former Yugoslavia), others for beef for soup (beef noodle soup is traditionally de rigeur at Sunday family lunches across Slovenia) or a rack of pork ribs.

The Ivanetič family butcher shop is a neighborhood generalist, with all manner of meat available. Miran is refreshingly down-to-earth, young and cool and easy-going and not the least bit neurotic. He is unprepossessing, despite being the favorite butcher of two of Slovenia's most famous chefs, but he does seem to be constantly thinking, knowledgeable, and a consummate professional, but with a vacation attitude towards work. He does what he does well and does not need to put on any airs and does not need to dip into marketing gimmicks. You want good meat? You know where to come, but you'll have to find him, because he's not going to shop himself around. That's the definition of cool.

———————

Slovenia does not have a celebrity butcher, but Miran comes close to that title. He is the personal butcher for JB, of course, and his other big client and now friend is chef Bine Volčič, who is Slovenia's most prominent TV chef personality, having hosted a popular cooking reality show and now hosting the local version of MasterChef. Providing meat for these two is as sexy a gig as a butcher can get. What is even more impressive is the faith which these chefs have in him. Once JB called him up and said he would need meat for 1,200 hamburgers. When asked exactly what he had in mind for them, JB simply told Miran "bring me whatever you think is best." That sort of faith is rare on the part of high-end chefs, who are often control freaks. JB is not. He believes that his favorite butcher will have the best sense of what meat to provide him with, and it would be presumptuous of him to make an order over the phone, without seeing and handling and tasting whatever was in the lockers at that moment. When asked about what JB orders on any given week, Miran laughs and says that he just tells him to bring him whatever he recommends.

The family butcher shop was established by Miran's parents, and he felt it was inevitable that he should take it over. He's a go-with-the-flow sort of guy. His approach to meat is similarly Taoist. He does not go in for any exotic mail-order animals. No Argentine or Danish steaks for him. No Wagyu or Angus, no kangaroo or ostrich. What Miran likes best is the best of whatever is local. This is precisely in line with JB's philosophy, and the philosophy of this book. So even though they might not be as objectively desirable as Wagyu or Angus, Miran likes to serve an indigenous breed of cow, Cika. When asked about its qualities, Miran smiles and shrugs. "It's nothing special," he says. It is not known for anything in particular and is most often just used as a milking cow. But this is part of his implicit point. It's all about how the meat is handled, its freshness and how it is cooked. This is all far more important than its origins or ancestry. "And isn't it better," he says calmly, "to eat the best of what's local, locally?" In Japan, he'd happily serve up Kobe beef, but it feels artificial, somehow wrong, to do so in Slovenia. He has a point.

He also has a point when he says that customers might come in for extra fancy cuts from extra fancy cows, but if they don't know how to cook them well, then it's essentially a waste. He'd rather sell them something local and give them some tips on how to cook it right, and he doesn't mind earning less money doing so, than try to be all fancy. There's a purity to this attitude that is refreshing.

There is an open secret that all meat buyers should know, but few do. The most important factor in the quality of the meat you eat is first what the meat you eat ate. That is logical enough. But the second most important is the level of calm of the animal just prior to its being killed. Miran can tell, just by looking at the meat, and certainly by touching it, whether the animal was stressed prior to its slaughter. Animals that are stressed prior to being killed have adrenaline flowing through their muscles. Meat is simply the muscle of animals and adrenaline-filled muscles contract. They are tighter and an entirely different color than the same muscles when relaxed. All of the butchers and farmers I spoke to assure me that meat from animals under stress before being killed is much worse, morally and in terms of taste. I would be curious to try the same cut of meat, prepared by the same butcher and cooked by the same chef in the same way, but from an animal killed at a generic but decent slaughterhouse, and one killed at home by its caring farmer. I am told that the difference is night and day.

It may sound funny coming from a butcher, but Miran says that we all eat too much meat. The problem is not the meat that we eat, but the quality. We tend to prefer the cheapest version we can find, but who knows where it comes from, Miran argues, and how it was handled and treated? We are used to eating lots and lots of mediocre meat. We tend not to notice this, for a few reasons. First is that, because we like our meat to be as cheap as possible, we are used to the taste of mediocre meat. It tastes fine to us and fine is good enough and it is what we've grown up with and are accustomed to. We also tend to hide the taste with elaborate spice mixes or sauces. If you have any habit of eating your meat "well done," then it is irrelevant whether you buy cheap or high-quality meats: if it is well done, it loses almost all of its taste and becomes only a texture. That is why chefs find it annoying when customers ask for their steak to be cooked well done. They are essentially asking the chef to remove all the taste from it. Yet we tend to find this acceptable, because we're used to overcooked meat covered in sauce, in which case all you taste is sauce and a meat-like texture. That's how meat was always served in Slovenia prior to JB's return from Austria.

The best steak should be chosen by a butcher who you visit regularly and feel you can rely on. Someone like Miran. It is worthwhile to choose a good butcher and become a regular. You'll want to know where the meat comes from, and local is inevitably better. Hopefully the animal that gave its life to sustain yours was killed in a humane way, for moral reasons and to ensure its maximum flavor. Then cook the meat the way it should be cooked. Don't cook red meat well done, because well done means it was not done well. Let the meat keep its flavor, Miran urges. Braise the tougher cuts if the recipe calls for it, but steaks and burgers, anything that can be cooked rare to medium rare, should be treated with respect, which means leave well done well enough alone.

I'll trust Miran on this one. The very best chefs in Slovenia, like JB, put 100 percent of their faith in him.

BEEF RIBS WITH HOMEMADE PLUM JAM, STEAMED BREAD, AND BABY CARROTS

BARLEY:

Wash the barley and cook in salted water for about 25 minutes. Drain the cooked grains and leave to dry on baking paper for 24 hours at room temperature. Quickly deep-fry in oil at 350°F (175°C), so the grains pop.

1¾ ounces (50 g) barley
Salt
Oil for deep-frying

RIBS:

Combine the tomato paste, olive oil, honey, and seasonings. Rub the ribs on all sides with this mixture.
Place the meat onto an oven rack, with a baking tray underneath to catch the juices. Place the wine, garlic, roughly chopped vegetables, and some water in the tray. Bake the ribs for 14 hours at 195°F (90°C). Check them occasionally and baste them with the juices from the tray.

1 tablespoon tomato paste
1 cup (200 ml) olive oil
3 tablespoons honey
Salt, coarsely ground pepper, 1 bay leaf
6½ pounds (3 kg) beef short ribs
1 cup (200 ml) Merlot
4 cloves garlic
1 carrot, roughly chopped
½ celeriac, roughly chopped
1 onion, roughly chopped
2 cups (400 ml) water

JAM:

Pit the plums and combine with the sugar and brandy. Simmer for two and a half hours, stirring constantly. Leave to cool.

¾ pound (400 g) plums
7 ounces (200 g) sugar
½ cup (100 ml) plum brandy

BREAD:

Crumble the yeast into the flour, add the salt and milk, and knead to form a dough. Leave to rise for half an hour, then knead again and leave to rise again. Divide into apricot-sized buns, leave to rise once more, and place into a steamer basket. Place the basket over a saucepan of simmering water, cover, and steam for 18 minutes.

⅔ ounce (20 g) fresh yeast
¾ pound (320 g) all-purpose flour
1 cup (200 ml) milk
Salt

CARROTS:

Wash the carrots well and fry in ghee for about 6 minutes or until crisp.

8 baby carrots
1 ounce (30 g) clarified butter (ghee)

TO SERVE:

Cut the ribs into pieces and arrange on a plate. Add some sauce, steamed bread, jam, carrots, and fried barley.

SEARED BEEF FILLET WITH BEEF SAUCE, MUSTARD MAYONNAISE, AND CAVIAR

———————————

Slice the fillet into ½-inch slices. Heat the olive oil in a frying pan and sear the slices, about 8 seconds on each side, then cut into approximately ¾-inch cubes. Marinate briefly with the oil from the pan and season with fleur de sel and pepper.

¾ pound (400 g) dry-aged beef fillet
½ cup (100 ml) olive oil
Fleur de sel
Coarsely ground pepper

SAUCE:
Slightly heat the demi-glace, add vinegar and oil, and stir.

1 cup (200 ml) beef demi-glace
1 tablespoon aged wine vinegar
¼ cup (50 ml) olive oil

MUSTARD MAYONNAISE:
Place the egg, salt, and pepper into a tall container and blend with an immersion blender. Slowly add the sunflower oil to create a mayonnaise. Finally add the mustard and blend until smooth.

1 egg
Salt and pepper
½ cup (100 ml) sunflower oil
¼ cup + 2 tablespoons (80 g) Dijon mustard

TO SERVE:
Pour the beef sauce onto a plate, then arrange the cubes of beef fillet on it. Dot the mustard mayonnaise around the fillet and decorate with caviar and radicchio.

7 ounces (200 g) sturgeon caviar
Young radicchio for decoration

JURE AND ALENKA AŽMAN.
COLT MEAT.

COLT MEAT

There is a theme I've come across while researching for this book. Just about everyone I spoke to who is in the world of butchery or raising animals to be consumed has a deep and heartfelt love for these animals. This seems incongruous with the fact that they raise them to be eaten. What might sound hypocritical as you read this comes across as nothing of the sort, when you see the expressions on the faces of these warm-hearted carnivores, who express genuine and deep concern for the welfare of the animals prior to, as they might say, "the big moment."

And so it is with Jure and his wife Alenka, who are proprietors of Slovenia's first fast food restaurant, which preceded the arrival of McDonald's and its ilk. Back in 1993, Jure was an enthusiastic ice hockey player and would play with his amateur team at the hockey rink in Tivoli Park, in the center of Ljubljana. After an evening of playing, he and his teammates would be hungry, and there was very little that was open late at night where they could get a meal. That gave them an idea to open a fast food establishment that would serve a very special type of meat that Alenka's family had been butchering for two generations. Alenka's father studied for two years in Germany to be a butcher, back during the time of Yugoslavia. When he returned home to Slovenia, he was told by the socialist government, which controlled these things, that there were enough butchers of more traditional meats, and that, if he wanted to register as a butcher, he would have to focus on horse meat. Accepting this, he turned around and spent another two years in Germany, training to be a horse butcher.

Horses have been consumed historically in almost all societies that have kept horses, but they were not raised for meat until relatively recently. In past centuries, horses were used ubiquitously for transport and for labor and for war. It was not the done thing to eat a horse that was otherwise healthy. Horse was considered the food of the poor and it was usually older horses or horses that had an injury that prevented them from being used as machines to assist humans, that they would be eaten. Thus, horse meat was considered secondary, an afterthought when the horse could no longer be used in the way one would wish. But with the advent of tractors and tanks and jeeps, horses essentially were retired from their previous duties.

"The only horses you see these days," Jure tells me, "are horses raised for food or a very small number for sport, as in racing or riding schools. There is the occasional horse kept as a sort of farm pet, but whenever you see a group of horses these days, they are being raised to be consumed." This is the darker side to the noble sight of an expansive pen in which horses frolic. In some societies nowadays, horse meat is considered taboo. Americans, for example, tend to object to eating an animal that they find cute or noble—this chapter might even prompt some outraged readers to pen a grumpy letter. But many countries take no issue in eating horse, like France, where it is ubiquitous. Slovenia is somewhere in between. It is not common here, but you're unlikely to find anyone who objects enough to write a grumpy letter. And in one format, horse meat is hugely popular. That is in burger format, as served at the Ažman's fast food restaurant, which they coyly named Hot Horse.

I ate at the Hot Horse the first time I was ever in Slovenia, while traveling as a student, so I was delighted to finally meet the couple behind the legendary kiosk that I have been patronizing for many years. Jure and Alenka are hyper-enthusiastic about their product and talk about eating horse meat so often that they find it refreshing when they'll go to a barbecue and someone throws chicken on the grill. For them, horse is a quotidian treat, but a treat, nonetheless. They are also extremely knowledgeable about the benefits of horse meat. Horses are incredibly clean and particular animals. They do not like to drink out of a container that another horse, or another person, has drunk out of. Colts are fed by their mother's milk for the first year, and are in utero for twelve months, meaning that there is no such thing as the sort of mass-produced horror show chicken farms in the world of horses. They must be free range, as they will simply die if they are taken too early from their mothers and not given room to run. This means that, out of necessity, horses are raised in a way that would be deemed organic and humane. They consume nothing that is unnatural, and so the meat has no allergens. Along with rabbit, it is recommended in Slovenia by doctors for people who have digestive issues with other meats. It also has a lot of water weight in it, which is considered a plus and shows that the animal has been healthy.

It has one of the highest levels of iron, so it is prescribed by doctors here for those suffering an iron deficiency, in lieu of taking supplement pills. It also has an ideal balance of omega-3 and omega-6 fatty acids. It is, the Ažmans tell me, the super meat, the leanest and healthiest of all red meats. It is something that you could eat many times a week without thinking twice about it. It also happens to be delicious, with a taste akin to lean beef. The only possible objection is the nobility factor. Some of us don't like the idea of eating horse, and that's that. But if you're a carnivore, this is the healthiest red meat you could choose.

Just about all of the horse meat consumed in the form of Hot Horse burgers or at restaurants like JB's comes from colts or foals, young male horses aged two to four years. Colt meat is the most tender and flavorful, while older horses produce meat that is less desirable and tends to go best made into sausages and dried products.

JB likes to take less fancy cuts of meat, and Alenka assures me that all the top chefs prefer cuts that are considered of lower quality, but which harness a lot of flavor. Anybody can throw a filet mignon on the grill and it's going to taste pretty good (provided it isn't overcooked), but chefs like to show their chops by taking the chops that are otherwise considered difficult to work with, like cheeks. Jure tells me that you really can't go wrong when cooking horse yourself. It should be at room temperature (not straight from the fridge) before cooking and should sizzle just briefly in the thickest, hottest pan you can get (preferably cast iron). What you don't want to do is let it cook by putting it in a pan that is not yet hot and having the temperature rise gradually.

There are almost no professional horse butchers in Slovenia, and only two of note in Ljubljana. There is one, Mesarstvo Krušič, that has a sort of secret, unmarked restaurant adjacent to it, in a residential neighborhood, and the other one is the Ažman's family establishment. They started their butchering business to provide burger patties for the Hot Horse but have since expanded and produce all manner of equine goodness: pate, steaks, sausages, salami, and even prepared meals, still most of them handmade by Alenka, like goulash and Bolognese and meatballs. But if you're a tourist in Ljubljana, you will surely have read about the Hot Horse burgers. It had a special box in my Lonely Planet Slovenia guidebook many years ago, and visiting it is still a "must-do" thing for visitors to the capital. A 24-hour horse burger stand is just fun and kooky enough for tourists to add it to their bucket list.

Don't think of Hot Horse as fast food in the industrial, mass-produced sense. This is the best sort of fast food, which is fast, but of controlled high quality and with a great love for detail and passion for the ingredients. Why I am writing so much about a fast food stand, in this book about JB's search for the best ingredients in Slovenia? It may seem incongruous that one of the world's best chefs would buy meat from a proprietor of a fast food kiosk, but it all makes sense when you taste those burgers. And here's the real surprise: when I ask Jure what cut of meat JB gets from him, to be served simply and purely, as carpaccio, he replies that JB gets the same meat that goes into Hot Horse burgers. One of the world's best chefs considers the meat that is ground up for fast food burgers to be the best in his country. That means your cheap and quick horse burger is made of the same raw materials as the high-end carpaccio at the most famous restaurant in the capital.

Jure enthusiastically hands me a dried smoked horse sausage packed with chilies, to eat like beef jerky. It's amazing. I don't find myself traumatized by the idea of eating horse when someone like Jure, who trained as a butcher after falling in love with Alenka and joining the family business, explains in a heartfelt way that this consumption of meat is something that we omnivorous humans are built to do. It is part of a natural cycle that has developed as long as humans have been humans. But even he cannot bring himself to actually butcher any animal, nor could that grandfather who trained as a butcher in Germany. In fact, not one of the top-drawer butchers and farmers featured in this book and visited while researching it could bring themselves to kill their own animals. These good people have a defense mechanism that I recognize in myself. When they get a quartered carcass from the slaughterhouse, it is sufficiently distanced from the idea of the animal that they love and respect that they can get on with business without being upset. But killing the animal is an entirely different story, and if they were obliged to kill the animals themselves, they would all be vegetarians. It might read as hypocritical, but it does not sound that way when you hear these stories straight from the horse's mouth, so to speak.

COLT CARPACCIO WITH POTATO CREAM, WILD HERB SAUCE, JERUSALEM ARTICHOKE, POMEGRANATE, AND RASPBERRY VINEGAR

Remove sinews from the meat and wrap it tightly in cling film. Place in the freezer for 40 minutes to freeze slightly. Using a meat slicer or mandoline, cut into extremely thin slivers, and arrange on plates.

1¾ pounds (800 g) colt meat (top round)

SAUCE:
Wash the meadow herbs and chop. Place into a food processor with the olive oil and two pinches of salt, and blend. Add the xanthan gum and blend again. Pass through a fine sieve to make a smooth green cream. If any lumps remain, or the oil separates, whisk until completely smooth.

5¼ ounces (150 g) mixed meadow herbs: narrowleaf plantain, dandelion greens, yarrow, wood sorrel, maidenstears
¼ cup (50 ml) olive oil
Salt
Tiny pinch (0.2 g) xanthan gum

POTATO CREAM:
Peel the potato and boil in salted water until soft. Place into a food processor with a little of the cooking water. Blend, adding the vinegar and olive oil, and season with salt and pepper to taste, until the cream is smooth.

1 potato, the size of a fist
2 tablespoons (30 ml) apple cider vinegar
¼ cup (50 ml) olive oil
Salt and pepper

Open the pomegranate and carefully remove the seeds.

1 pomegranate

JERUSALEM ARTICHOKE:
Carefully peel the Jerusalem artichokes and cut the flesh into tiny cubes, approximately the size of pomegranate seeds. Cook the peels for 15 minutes in salted water on low heat. Dehydrate the peels in a convection oven for 4 hours at 150°F (65°C). Heat the oil to 350°F (175°C) and quickly fry the peels, dipping each piece into the oil for 2 seconds.

3 ounces (80 g) Jerusalem artichoke
2¼ cups (500 ml) oil for deep-frying

TO SERVE:
Top the meat slices on plates with pomegranate seeds, Jerusalem artichoke cubes, herb sauce, and potato cream. Drizzle with raspberry vinegar and olive oil, season with fleur de sel and coarsely ground pepper, and finally decorate with some fresh wild herbs and fried Jerusalem artichoke peels.

Raspberry vinegar
Olive oil
Fleur de sel
Coarsely ground pepper
Fresh wild meadow herbs

HOW TO MAKE RASPBERRY VINEGAR:
Place the raspberries (about 7 ounces, or 200 grams) into a plastic container, close and leave in the fridge for a month or until they go sour. Then mash the berries and squeeze through a kitchen gauze, to obtain raspberry vinegar.

NOTE:
The meat must be sliced at least 10 minutes before arranging the other ingredients on the plate, so that it warms to room temperature.

COLT CHEEKS WITH GROUND-IVY, POTATO DUMPLINGS WITH COTTAGE CHEESE, AND FENNEL JAM

Remove the skins from the cheeks and reserve the trimmings. Season the cheeks with salt and pepper. Heat the oil in a pan and sear the cheeks quickly but thoroughly to brown. Set aside and keep warm. Place the trimmings into the pan in which the cheeks were seared, together with the chopped shallots, and fry for 10 minutes. Add the wine and beef stock, stir, then return the cheeks to the pan and cover. Add the herbs and simmer on very low heat for 2 hours and 15 minutes. Turn the meat occasionally. Do not stir but rather shake the pan and add water if the sauce is becoming too dry. When the cheeks are tender, remove them from the pan and strain the sauce without mashing the solids. Reduce the strained sauce for 5 minutes, then return the cheeks to the sauce to keep warm.

2 colt cheeks
(together approx. 1½ pounds or 600 g)
¾ cup (150 ml) sunflower oil
10½ ounces (300 g) shallots, chopped
1½ cups (300 ml) Merlot
1½ cups (300 ml) beef stock
Salt, black peppercorns, 1 bay leaf, thyme

DUMPLINGS:
Peel the potatoes and boil in salted water until soft. Pass through a sieve. Add the butter and the egg yolk, mix, add the flour, and knead to form dough.
Knead the cheese until it is soft and form into four ¾-inch balls.
Take a piece of dough the size of an apricot, flatten it in your palm, place a ball of cheese in the middle, and form into a dumpling, sealing the edges well. Repeat with remaining dough and cheese to make three more dumplings.
Place the dumplings into salted boiling water and cook for 15 minutes.

⅓ pound (150 g) potatoes
1 ounce (30 g) butter
1 egg yolk
½ cup (100 g) all-purpose flour
½ cup (100 g) cottage cheese

GROUND-IVY POWDER:
Pick the ground-ivy leaves from stems (you should get 1¾ ounces or 50 g). Reserve some fresh leaves for garnish and dry the rest at room temperature for approximately 2 days or in the oven for 2 hours at 160°F (70°C). When dry, grind to a powder in a coffee grinder. Melt the butter in a pan and add the ground-ivy powder. When well-combined, roll the dumplings in the butter.

½ cup (100 g) ground-ivy
1 ounce (30 g) butter

FENNEL JAM:
Wash the fennel and chop fine. Place into a pan with the kombucha, add the sugar, and cook on low heat, stirring regularly, for an hour and a half, to make the jam. If it becomes too thick, add a little more kombucha.

5¼ ounces (150 g) fennel
½ cup (100 ml) kombucha
¼ cup + 2 tablespoons (80 g) sugar

TO SERVE:
Cut the cheeks into ½-inch slices. Pour the sauce over the top and add a few of the remaining ground-ivy leaves. Add a dumpling and a spoon of fennel jam.

NOTE:
Sear the meat well, as the crust is very important for the taste, as well as for retaining the juices. In addition, we are left with an excellent base for the sauce in the pan.

GORAZD KOCBEK.
PUMPKIN SEED OIL.

PUMPKIN SEED OIL

The room exudes an aura of green. It's a beautiful color, but its shade is amorphous. At times it appears like grass, sometimes like moss, at times like oiled leather. The walls are brushed with a mossy spray, the mist and scent of the hundreds of millions of pumpkin seeds that have been processed here and made into what is almost certainly the world's best pumpkin seed oil. The room exudes an age and dignity of mechanical manual labor, the opposite of a sterile factory, producing something delicious that those involved are in love with.

There are 825 varieties of pumpkins around the world, and only one of them is suitable for making pumpkin seed oil. *Cucurbita pepo* var. *styriaca* or Styrian pumpkins are native to the swath of land that runs from Prekmurje, in northwestern Slovenia, across the border into Styria, southern Austria. It is an entirely local product, and one I'd never encountered before moving to Slovenia. Used locally to dress salads, it is rich, earthy, toasty, a nice compliment, or alternative, to using olive oil. Gorazd Kocbek and his family have been making it since 1929, processing this tsunami of seeds using the same, century-old mechanical presses that were originally purchased and used by Alojz Kocbek, Gorazd's grandfather. In the heat of this green-tinged workshop, an elegant old man stirs the toasting seeds, before they are loaded into a stamper which presses the juices out, leaving a patty of dried, smashed seeds, which is used as feed for livestock, in a process with no waste whatsoever. JB likes to use pumpkin seed oil as some would chocolate sauce, to top homemade gelato, but that is only the start.

We are in the pressing room of Gorazd's family pumpkin seed company. In this very same room, Grandpa Alojz started the family's business. Gorazd is proud that he uses the same machines that his grandfather bought off of another farmer, so they are likely far older than a century. Only light updates were made to this room—a fresh set of tiles on the wall and a few parts changed here and there, as necessary. These same machines are still chugging away, a steamy steampunk fantasyland of gears and greased metal and levers and heat and that delicious toasted scent that is difficult to place, unless you know the end product being made here.

Styrian pumpkin seed oil is still exotic in most parts of the world and it is difficult to describe. It is dark, treacle-colored, appearing like fine balsamic vinegar, but it is certainly an oil, slick over the tongue and like unfiltered olive oil in consistency. It has a warm, toasted taste, with walnut oil as perhaps the closest in comparison, and yet it is its own marvelous, shining product.

What seems a niche, quotidian product is here elevated to unimagined heights. Gorazd is an expert when it comes to marketing and design and has made this everyday peasant condiment into something high-end, in terms of taste and look. He has even produced a luxury version, in a specially-designed cut glass decanter and leather box, which is a hit among Arabian royalty. His pumpkins are harvested from nearby fields, and around 20,000–30,000 liters are made for his own bottling, while he processes that much again for other local farmers who bring their seeds to him for handling. The seeds must be cleaned and dried the day pumpkins are harvested, otherwise they go bad. Once processed, and stored in a dry and cold space, they can last for up to two years. But they don't sit around that long, as just a few specialized workers, with fingernails and palms stained that lovely iridescent velvet green, work them through machines, using every bit, scrap, and drop. The flesh of the Styrian pumpkins is not considered tasty, but it is reused to become compost for its own fields. The discarded parts of the shell are pressed into oversized hockey pucks of dry waste material that is beloved of cows and fish, and therefore becomes feed.

It takes 33 average-sized pumpkins, containing around 6½ pounds (3 kg) of seeds, to produce one liter of oil. With that in mind, one should look askance at cut-priced oils and consider this to be a luxury product, along the lines of the highest-end olive oils and balsamic vinegars from Modena. Most of the underpriced competition use imported Chinese pumpkin seeds, which cost half as much and have to travel the world, leaving a nasty carbon footprint, to reach the producer. Sometimes there is no pumpkin seed at all in the "pumpkinseed oil," just an extract. Believe me, you want the original, from the original location. Gorazd explains that you can get good pumpkin seed oil in Australia, as some farmers there bought Slovenian seeds to plant them in Antipodean soil. He tried the result and it was very good, but different. The soil, the terroir, makes the product as much as the seed and the farmer's good intentions. It is logical that the pumpkins will thrive best where nature first established them. The Kocbek lineup includes cold-pressed (never reaching a temperature higher than 105°F, or 40°C), stone-ground, and the more traditional steel-ground, as well as a "bio" line, though having inspected the family operation thoroughly, I can report that everything they make is as bio as can be, by any standards.

It is no surprise that Gorazd has collaborated with the other great master of oil featured in this cookbook, Gregor Lisjak. They are a fitting match, as both are young, movie star handsome, and have a charisma in presentation and true love for their product that is infectious. They also nicely bracket Slovenia, with Gorazd on the far eastern end, and Gregor on the far western. They collaborated on an ideally-proportioned salad dressing of olive and pumpkin seed oil. All of Slovenia in one bottle.

Gorazd uses his own oil for salads, of course, but he also uses it as a cooking oil, which is something that hadn't occurred to me. Dishes cooked on a fat of pumpkin seed oil will turn a lovely dark color, which imparts that beautiful toasted flavor to eggs or fish or steak. It's not just a topping. It can also stand alone as a sauce for otherwise undressed pasta. Gorazd's favorite way to taste it is his mother's recipe, mixing *skuta* (a fresh curd cheese, like a more sophisticated version of cottage cheese), whipped through with pumpkin seed oil, and toasted, chopped pumpkin seeds. It is spooned onto grilled bread. I can attest to the fact that Mama Kocbek knows what she's doing.

JB, like most great chefs, is known for unusual approaches to ingredients. But with some in this cookbook, his desire for purity and honoring the ingredient shines through to the point of preferring to use it in its raw form. Witness his serving of Krško polje prosciutto. He'll cook with it, but he wants his guests to taste it unadulterated, just sliced with thin precision and served. It's the same with Kocbek pumpkin seed oil. "I prefer to use pumpkin seed oil at the end, as the dot on the I," he says. And when the dot is this good, I can see why.

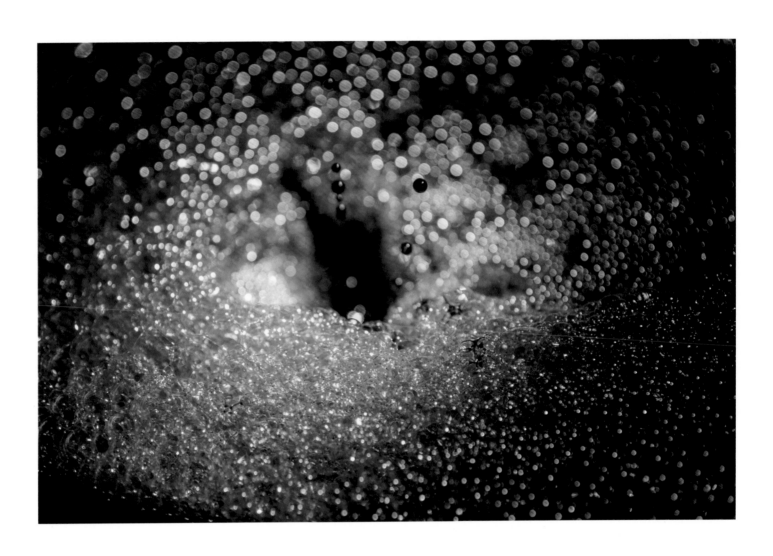

VEAL TERRINE WITH PUMPKIN SEED OIL, RED AND WHITE SAUCE, AND SHEATHED WOODTUFT MUSHROOMS

TERRINE:

Place the meat, vegetables, and herbs in a saucepan and add enough hot water to cover. Cook, covered, on a low heat for 1 hour, then uncover and cook a further 40 minutes. When the meat is cooked, remove the bone (shoulder blade) and cut the meat into small pieces. Cut the carrot and celeriac that were cooked with the meat into small pieces and add to the cubes of meat. Strain the soup.
Soak the gelatin leaves in cold water.
Cool half the stock to use for the sauce. Heat the remaining stock and add to the meat and vegetables to obtain a thick mixture. Squeeze excess water from the gelatin and add to the mixture. Stir well and transfer to silicone trays. Ensure that the meat, vegetables, and stock are evenly distributed. Place in the fridge for 3 hours.

1⅔ pounds (750 g) veal shoulder, bone-in
1 carrot
1 onion
½ celeriac
1 bunch parsley
Black peppercorns
1 bay leaf
1 sprig lovage
4 teaspoons gelatin powder (4 g gelatin leaves)

WHITE SAUCE:

Place the egg, vinegar, stock, mustard, salt and pepper into a tall container. Blend with an immersion blender and slowly add the sunflower oil to obtain a smooth emulsion.

1 egg
2 tablespoons apple cider vinegar
½ cup (100 ml) stock (from terrine)
1 teaspoon mustard
Salt
Pepper
¾ cup (150 ml) sunflower oil

RED SAUCE:

Blanch the tomato, peel, and cut into small pieces. Place into a tall container, add ½ cup (100 ml) stock remaining from the terrine, season with salt to taste and blend with an immersion blender. Slowly add the oil to obtain an emulsion, then pass through a fine sieve.

1 tomato
½ cup (100 ml) stock (from terrine)
Salt
½ cup (100 ml) sunflower oil

PARSNIP:

Cut the parsnip into very thin slices using a mandoline. Place the slices onto kitchen towels and leave for half an hour to dry slightly. Fry in oil at 325°F (165°C), to obtain chips.

1 parsnip
Oil for deep-frying

BRUSSELS SPROUTS:

Remove the outer leaves and separate each individual leaf, then quickly blanch in salted boiling water.

4 Brussels sprouts

TO SERVE:

Carefully remove the cooled terrines from the trays and put onto a plate. Distribute some white and red purées so there is some on the plate and some on the terrine. Combine the lettuce, Brussels sprout leaves, and cress in a bowl, add some red sauce, and toss to marinate.
Place the marinated salad on the plate, add the mushrooms and fried parsnip, and finally drizzle with pumpkin seed oil.

Lettuce leaves
Watercress
3½ ounces (100 g) pickled sheathed woodtuft mushrooms (in vinegar)
½ cup (100 ml) pumpkin seed oil

BOILED VEAL TONGUE WITH SHEEP RICOTTA, GORICA RADICCHIO, AND PUMPKIN SEED OIL

Place the veal tongue into a pan and add enough water to cover, add the vegetables and herbs, and cook on low heat for 15 minutes. Take the cooked tongue from the stock and leave to cool. Reserve the stock. Thin slice with a meat slicer or mandoline.

1 fresh veal tongue
½ onion
1 small carrot
½ celeriac
1 sprig parsley
1 bay leaf
Salt, black peppercorns

RICOTTA:
Blend ricotta and sour cream with some salt and caraway with an immersion blender until smooth. Fill a piping bag with the mixture.

6½ ounces (180 g) fresh sheep ricotta
2¼ ounces (60 g) sour cream
Salt
Pinch of ground caraway

RADICCHIO:
Heat the oil in a frying pan and briefly fry the radicchio heads (2 minutes). Take off the heat and cover the pan, so that the radicchio cooks a little and releases its juices.

¼ cup (50 ml) olive oil
4 heads Gorica radicchio
Salt and pepper

TO SERVE:
Put the warm radicchio on a plate. Fill the tongue slices with the ricotta cream and roll to make roulades, and place on the radicchio. Spoon some radicchio juices on top. Mix the pumpkin seed oil with the stock. Drizzle some of this marinade on top of the dish and use the rest to marinate dandelion leaves and turnip greens. Finally garnish with marinated leaves.

3 tablespoons pumpkin seed oil
½ cup (100 ml) stock
(from cooking the tongue)
Dandelion leaves and turnip greens to decorate

SAMO KUPLJEN,
VINO KUPLJEN.
WINE.

WINE

▇▇▇▇▇

Samo Kupljen knows how to live. This is immediately clear when we sit down at his restaurant, which floats on a hilltop above the endlessly lovely rolling hills of Slovenia's Jeruzalem. I'm a bit embarrassed to say that I had no awareness that this part of the country existed. We are in the farthest-flung region, in the triangle of the Austrian, Croatian, and Hungarian border, about as far away as one can drive from where I live, near the capital, while still remaining in the country. By Slovenian standards, a two-hour drive is long. But I thought that this region was totally flat, populated by gypsies and storks and mill wheels slowly churning along rivers. I did not expect something resembling Provence or Tuscany, with one perfectly-domed hill after another, each strewn with green vines and dotted with milk-white cattle, the French breed Charolais, it turns out, as if some seventeenth century Provencal landscape painter had assembled it all as an ideal backdrop.

Samo tells us that the unusual name of this town dates back to 1381 when, as a form of pension, knights engaged in the Crusades were given parcels of land to cultivate and tax in this lush valley. The crusader knights carried with them relics from the Holy Land which, depending on your point of view, they either took as souvenirs or pillaged. For the sake of charm, let's say that they took them as souvenirs. Each hilltop is named after a saint: Saint Florian, Saint Martin . . .

The restaurant in which we sit is a part of Samo's small empire. He is a *bon vivant*, someone who enjoys the good life and gets every last drop out of it. He also pays attention to detail in a way that is surprising for someone who is wealthy and successful. He is in charge of all of the stores in the German Bauhaus home and construction supply super chain throughout the Balkans. But he's no mere businessman. He takes an enthusiastic interest in details and what they symbolize. For instance, this restaurant is built of only three primary materials: wood, sandstone, and glass, all local. Sandstone is symbolic because this whole lush area was once beneath the ocean, back in prehistoric times—fossilized sea life is still regularly discovered. The result is that the soil is ideal for growing grapes. Anyone who has not tried Slovenian wines will be pleasantly surprised, but those in the know, wine experts, oenophiles, and critics, are well aware that Slovenia is among the top wine producers in the world, in quality if not in quantity. So, it's no bad thing, inhaling this view and sipping from Samo's cellar.

Within an hour of meeting the man, I feel like I'm learning a lot from Samo, and not just about how to drink wine. I'll admit, while I'm an enthusiast, I don't know *how* to drink wine (I mean, I don't pour it into my ear, but I'm no aficionado). He does have a few tips with which JB concurs. Always smell deeply first before sipping. Good wines always smell good, and a bad odor will guarantee a bad taste. But sometimes the taste disappoints after the inhalation, while sometimes it exceeds the expectation. The very best wines match the quality of the scent and the taste perfectly, satisfying the high expectation of the former with the run-over-your-tongue of the latter.

Samo has casually arranged an elaborate multicourse meal with wine pairings from his vineyard for us but does so with an effortless class that distinguishes him. He makes no mention of his largess, of the number of courses, of how prized his restaurant is, of which awards his wines have won. Everything just happens, and wonderfully, and he has the confidence to present without the need to underscore and emphasize and sing his own praises. This is a man of poise. His wines match, particularly those in his playful Stars of Styria collection, each named after a constellation. *Star Wars* fans, there's a Skywalker wine, Samo's first red cuvee (90 percent Merlot with a touch of Pinot Noir and Blaufrankisch). I'm not sure how many oenophiles are also the sort who go out for Halloween dressed as Chewbacca, but for those who do, this is the wine for you. For my money, Loona, an unfiltered lemon-colored sauvignon that enjoys a four-week maceration, before maturing in 60-gallon (225-liter) French barrels, is like sipping sunshine. "With meat, beef, I like to drink and add to the sauce a Merlot," JB says. "If I use white wine, I want to use Rebula with meat. It has the most neutral taste. The sweeter wines I like best are Yellow Muscat or Riesling." So, if we were obliged to choose only one Kupljen wine, it would be his dry Riesling, but in practice, JB will enthusiastically use and serve them all.

Our next stop is Samo's vineyard, which looks like it was modeled on a French chateau. Samo comes from a family that is as close to aristocracy as Slovenia gets. Slovenia is refreshingly free of classism in the traditional sense that we associate, for instance, with England. The aristocracy was almost exclusively Germanic and imported along with the Habsburg rule. When the Habsburgs were ousted, the aristocrats left with them. This means that class distinctions are almost entirely earned, or occasionally, though not in this case, finagled by those who cleverly surfed the socialist political waters during the time of Yugoslavia. Samo's family have been influential because of what they have done, not because of how they were born, dating back generations.

The Kupljen vineyard has a high-tech cellar, as well as an adjacent one that looks medieval, complete with frescoes and religious objects covered in cobwebs, perched on enormous oaken casks that age the numerous wines he produces. Matjaž winds up getting Samo to straddle one of the enormous oak casks, as if he were riding a wooden bull, but it is an incongruous pose and they soon switch to something more noble.

One of my favorite things that Samo mentions, he does only in passing. Not long ago, he decided to dedicate himself to learning. He had such fun in his student days, studying around the globe with impeccable German, Serbo-Croatian, and English and, missing those days, trying to keep his mind nicely elastic, he decided to dedicate each year to hyper-specializing in one subject that he would learn thoroughly and deeply. One year it was sushi. He wanted to know everything there was to know about sushi, not only how to make it and its history, but every tiny detail. He is eager to share what he learned: he tells me with glee that, in Japan, it is illegal to export rice, as it is considered a national treasure. Therefore, the rice in Japan will always be special, even though Japanese varieties are grown elsewhere too. He took a microscope to the vinegar that's added to the rice, to the types of seaweed, to the knives used, even seeking out one of the knife-makers who caters to the most famous of sushi chefs. This type of hyper-analysis and eternal studentdom appeals to me immensely, but I lack the wallet to do it justice the way Samo does. His year of learning about sushi involved flights to Japan and bookings at every sushi restaurant that tickled his fancy. He orders all the best ingredients shipped to him. No expenses are spared, but you can see that this is an act of great passion. He spent another year just studying beef. That pasture of milk-white cattle that we can see from our table at his restaurant turns out to be his. Not only does he study the butchering and aging of meat, but he became a sort of amateur zoologist specializing in cows during one of his years of magical learning.

When I grow up, I hope to live like Samo. And I wouldn't mind creating, or at least drinking, the sort of wine that he produces, either.

CHICKEN IN WHITE WINE WITH ROOT VEGETABLES AND NEW POTATOES

Wash the chicken and rub with salt inside and out.

Heat the oven to 250°F (120°C).

Place the cleaned and roughly chopped vegetables and potatoes into a large copper or cast iron casserole dish together with the salt, peppercorns, and bay leaf. Stir well, add the oil, stock, and wine and place the chicken on top.

Cover and place in the oven for 1 hour. Check occasionally and baste the chicken with the juices from the bottom of the dish.

Uncover the pan, increase the temperature to 295°F (145°C), and roast a further 50 minutes to get nice crispy skin. Remove the bay leaf, and serve in the pot.

4½ pounds (2 kg) whole chicken (farm-raised)
½ celeriac
1 black radish, roughly chopped
1 turnip, roughly chopped
1 carrot, roughly chopped
5 small new potatoes, roughly chopped
1 red onion, roughly chopped
3 cloves garlic, roughly chopped
Salt
1 bay leaf
10 peppercorns
½ cup (100 ml) sunflower oil
1 cup (200 ml) chicken stock
1½ cups (300 ml) dry Šipon wine (also known as Furmint)

FOIE GRAS IN COGNAC SAUCE WITH DRIED APRICOT PURÉE AND RIESLING JELLY

Fry the foie gras on both sides without adding fat. Add the orange juice, cognac, and veal stock. Cook for 2 minutes, then remove the foie gras from the pan and keep warm. Add the frozen butter to the sauce and whisk briskly until smooth. Strain, add the foie gras, and keep warm for 3 minutes.

4 slices foie gras, approx. 3½ ounces or 100 g each
Juice of 1 orange
1⅓ tablespoons (20 ml) cognac
½ cup (100 ml) veal stock
3½ tablespoons (50 g) frozen butter

APRICOT PURÉE:
Cook the dried apricots with the water and wine for 10 minutes. Process to obtain a smooth apricot purée.

3 ounces (80 g) unsulphured dried apricots
½ cup (100 ml) water
½ cup (100 ml) Riesling

WINE JELLY:
Cook the wine, agar agar, and sugar on low heat for 5 minutes, then pour onto a silicone mat to obtain a thin sheet of wine jelly. When firm, use a biscuit cutter to cut out 4-inch circles.

½ cup (100 ml) Riesling
1 teaspoon (2 g) agar agar
1 ounce (30 g) sugar

TO SERVE:
Place the foie gras on a plate, add the sauce, and place a circle of jelly on top. Add the apricot purée, sprinkle with fleur de sel, and decorate with shiso leaves.

Shiso leaves
Fleur de sel

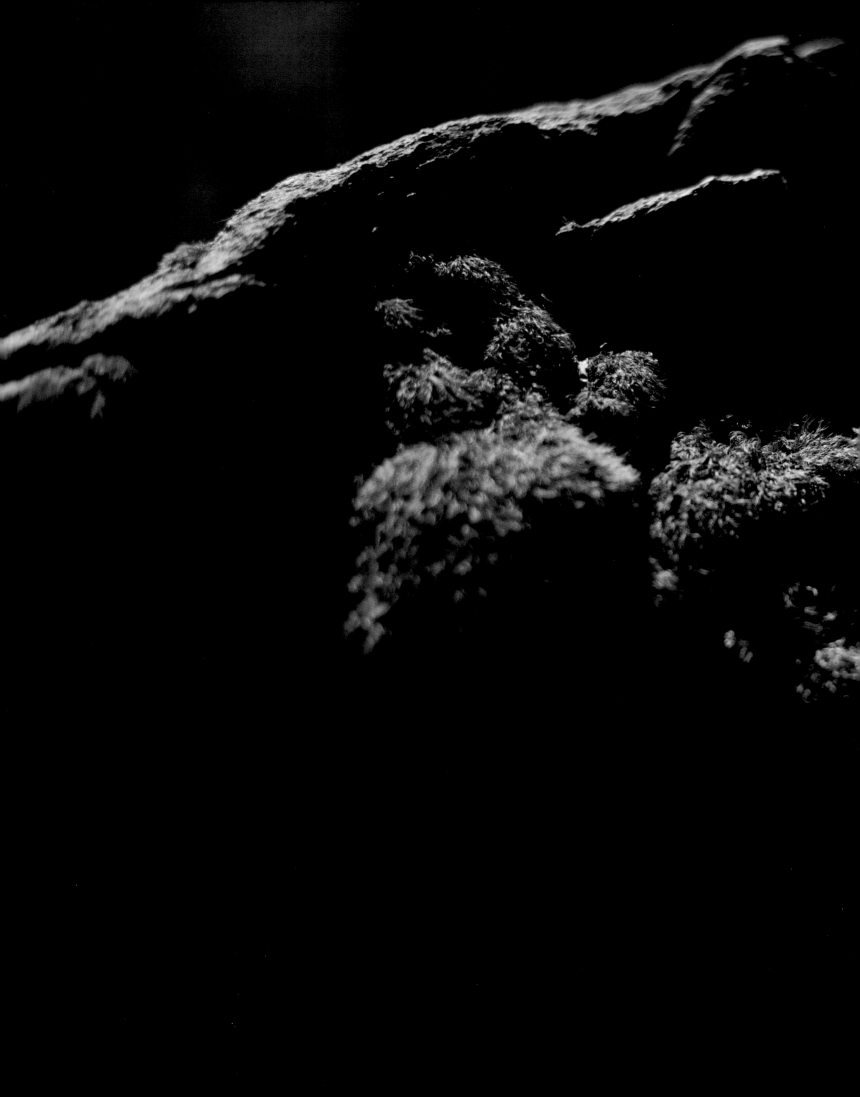

NIMROD.
GAME.

GAME

——————

Imagine one of the nicest people you ever met. Now imagine that person slitting
open the throat of a freshly-killed chamois and drinking the gushing blood. With that
little image in mind, I'd like you to meet my friend, Nejc. Nejc is a former president
of the Alpine region of Slovenian association of hunters, *lovci* or *jagri* as they are
known in this part of the world, the latter coming from their Austrian neighbors.
Let me stress that Nejc is a great lover of nature. This is one of the first things that
surprised me, as an American with a rather different and less flattering cliché about
what it means to be a hunter. Hunters in the Austrian-Slovenian tradition are more
like forest rangers than the American image of automatic weapon-toting, pickup
truck-driving, mullet-wearing, sleeveless flannel shirt-decked, Bud Light-drinking,
deer-in-headlight-chasing nogoodniks. Not to cast any aspersions.

——————

No, the tradition of hunters in this region is rich and long and deep and imbued with
a genuine love for nature and for animals. Anyone who objects to hunting should
also keep this in mind: the Slovenian Ministry of Forests, based on environmental
studies, requires that a certain number of each species of animal be culled each
year, in order to maintain an ideal balance within the ecosystem of the country.
That means that a certain number of bears, wolves, foxes, badgers, dormice,
chamois, mountain ibex, wild boar, and much more *must* be killed, by order of the
ecologists who work at the ministry. These scientists determine which species are
over-populated and the hunters provide what is essentially a national service. It
is also a sport, and a rich cultural tradition, but each of the kills must be reported
to the authorities. The meat for each kill must be paid for, as these animals are
effectively owned by the state, considered a national natural resource. And the
hunters are carefully overseen by local presidents, like Nejc. They are very careful
never to exceed their designated portion of prizes, but they are also careful to
fulfill the order of the ministry. They take what they do seriously, as a way to
maintain a balance in nature.

This is so different from the American stereotype of hunters that it takes a while for
it to sink in for me. There are tree-hugging scientists and ministry officials who lay
out exactly what the hunters' targets are each year–it sounds like a contradiction
in terms, considering the American and indeed British ideas of hunting. That means
that, when the ministry says that there should be a cull of 116 bears throughout
Slovenia in a recent year, that doing so is for the greater good, and not a simple
pastime or whimsy of gun-toting enthusiasts.

Nejc exudes kindness and a true love for the natural world. He is also a wonderful
host. After posing for the photos in the traditional army-green uniform that recalls
lederhosen (knee-high socks, roomy knee-length britches, a tweed jacket, a jaunty
green Robin-Hood-style cap with a badge featuring a mountain ibex pinned upon
it), Nejc leads us up a densely-forested mountain and down a steep path, weaving
between primary growth trees, to a tiny wooden cabin, his weekend getaway. Just
a single room, its walls ringed with benches, an ornately-carved table laid with a
pristine white tablecloth, little more. Outside, he sits upon one tree stump and pulls
over another, which has been converted into a makeshift table and cutting board.
Out comes a beautifully-crafted hunting knife, its handle made of a buck's antler.
Then the venison sausages: his own meat, his own kill, his own preparation. But he's
got a trick up his sleeve, or rather beneath his feet. There is what appears to be a slab
of wood on the pine-needle-lined earth. In fact, it is a hidden icebox, containing a
bottle of Nejc's own homemade schnapps, and a pair of shot glasses, attached to the
icebox lid, so they can never be lost. This party is just getting started.

Nejc's early interest in hunting developed as a young boy by going with his uncle,
an active *lovec*, hunter. He is the sort of hunter who takes greater pleasure in
strolling through the forests or spending a few hours seated quietly in a hunting
lookout, rather than actually shooting anything. His decision to become a hunter
was one that cannot be taken lightly. It takes years to get a hunting license, and you
have to pass quite rigorous tests which involve questions about the natural world
and forestry, laws, and animal anatomy, in order to qualify. Not everyone passes,
and it takes of good deal of effort, along the lines of completing a school degree.
Shooting animals is absolutely the least of it, and the thing that Slovenian hunters
do least frequently, among their activities.

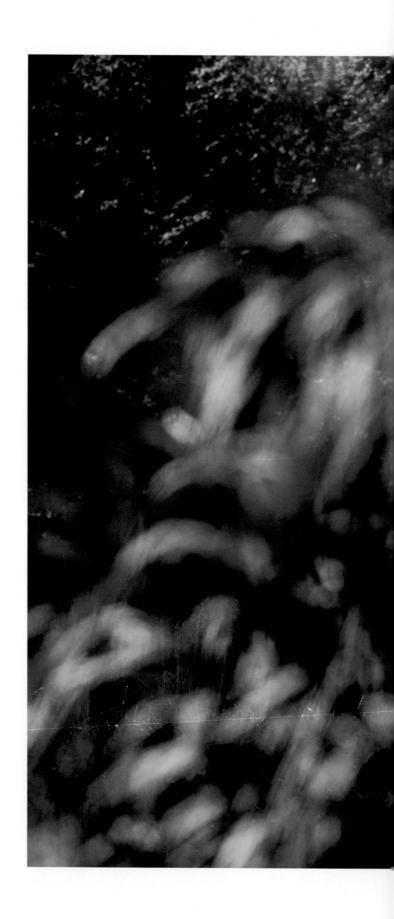

The traditions associated with the killing of quarry are surprisingly noble and Romantic. Nejc explains that, after an animal has been shot, you should place a branch in its mouth, to symbolically give it what is called "the last bite." A way of honoring the animal and giving thanks for its having given its life in order for us to sustain ours, this tradition dates back to our proto-human ancestors, when hunting was a sort of religious ritual and it really was a matter of survival, without farmed meats to turn to for sustenance. It is also an informal tradition to drink the blood of the first creature you kill as a newly-licensed hunter, hence that image of Nejc drinking the gushing blood of his freshly-downed chamois. The idea that the animal has a spirit and should be respected and given a respectful death is important to Nejc, as he almost tears up when talking about the animals he has killed. There's nothing sporty or macho about it.

The game meat that is featured in this chapter is the one likely to be considered the most exotic for just about anyone outside of Slovenia, because in many countries it is illegal to hunt bear or serve bear meat. A famous Slovenian chef and friend of JB was invited to cook a dinner across the border in Italy and wanted to feature bear. He was stopped at the border and the meat confiscated—it turned into a vegetarian dinner, by necessity. Slovenia is one of the only places that you can legally try specialties featuring bear.

This chapter is a bit of an outlier, because Nejc is not necessarily the provider of JB's bear meat. JB gets his game meat from a family-run, but not-insignificantly-sized company called Nimrod. But Nimrod gets its meat from hunters like Nejc. Because Nimrod is a well-run, but not quite as engaging or romantic company to feature in this chapter, we instead profiled the sort of hunter who provides meat to the company (and who is a good deal more photogenic than a walk-in meat freezer), which then processes it and ensures its quality, before passing it on to customers, most of them restaurants.

JB has some very enthusiastic customers from Austria, for instance, who asked him to call them whenever he has bear on the menu, which is just a few times a year, when hunters make it available to him. They'll drive down several hours from Austria to feast on their favorite, a dish that is a bit too gruesome-looking for my taste, but I am told it is delicious: bear paw. JB cooks bear in much the way one would beef, but bear, he says, is quicker to cook and softer in texture, a distinctive delicacy.

The most traditional dish for hunters to prepare, and the centerpiece of gatherings of hunters as part of this formalized and ritualistic national society, is goulash. This is a slowly-cooked stew that is best made in enormous quantities in a witchy iron cauldron hanging over an open fire and bubbling for hours. A good trick is to have an equal weight of chopped onions to meat—far more onions than seems logical. Dusted liberally with smoked paprika and packed with several types of meat, this is crazy good, and I love the sense of camaraderie and tradition involved in sitting with friends around a fire in a clearing in the woods, something our ancient ancestors did in much the same way.

Slovenia is an unusual country in that it has too much forest. That will sound funny, because we are used to hearing about countries that cut down their forests far too quickly, so deforestation is a more resonant issue than over-forestation (if that is even a term). But Slovenia has a wealth of square miles of forests per capita (62 percent of the country is forested, and the population is only two million, with 97 people per square kilometer, or 252 per square mile), and the forests can actually encroach on farm land. Thus, logging is acceptable and actually encouraged, within ministry-regulated limitations, as is hunting the beasts of the forest. These rich forests mean a rich natural world, full of animals who can be converted into some surprising specialties in the hunter tradition.

Consider the badger, which I imagine you *could* eat, but I'd never heard of as a specialty. According to Nejc and JB, who by now have finished off most of the venison sausage (and the hidden bottle of schnapps), it is an acquired taste, as is dormouse. Dormouse is something of a national specialty, by which I mean that it is a traditional thing to eat, but it is not a traditional thing to love eating. There is a dormouse food festival every year, but I'm told that the meat is rather sinewy and stringy, and the animal's rat-like appearance does not win it many lovers. A chapter in this book on dormice might have been a good conversation piece, and if JB features it (perhaps with a side of badger) on his menu one day when I'm in town, I'll gladly give it a try. Tradition is tradition. But me, I'll stick with the bear.

BRAISED BEAR PAWS
IN SAUCE AND BAKED APPLES

Sear the bear paws lightly in oil and keep warm. Fry the cleaned and roughly chopped vegetables in the same oil for about 15 minutes. Finally add the spices, crushing the juniper berries a little.

Pour the stock into the pan with the vegetables and add the bear paws. Cover and braise for 3 hours and 15 minutes. Stir and shake the pan occasionally, making sure that the vegetables and meat do not stick to the bottom. When the paws are tender, remove them from the pan and keep warm.

Remove the bay leaf, then process the vegetables in a food processor or Thermomix to a smooth purée. To obtain a smoother texture, pass through a sieve.

APPLES:
Wash, halve, and core the apples, brush with butter, sprinkle with sugar, and bake for 20 minutes at 325°F (165°C).

TO SERVE:
Place a paw on a plate, add the sauce, and a baked apple half.

4 bear paws
2 onions
1¾ ounces (50 g) rutabaga, roughly chopped
1¾ ounces (50 g) celeriac, roughly chopped
1¾ ounces (50 g) carrots, roughly chopped
1 cup (200 ml) oil
1 bay leaf
10 peppercorns
2 star anise
5 juniper berries
6½ cups (1.5 L) beef stock

2 apples
3 tablespoons (40 g) butter
2½ ounces (70 g) sugar

RED DEER FILLET WITH
JUNIPER BERRY SAUCE,
TARRAGON "ŠTRUKELJ,"
RED SWISS CHARD STEMS,
CELERIAC, AND CRANBERRY JAM

Bone the meat, remove the tendons, and chop the bones as finely as possible. Put the meat aside but keep it at room temperature, covered with plastic wrap.
Heat the oven to 360°F (180°C) and roast the bones and tendons for 25 minutes.

2¾ pounds (1.2 kg) venison back, on the bone
Fleur de sel
3 ounces (80 g) clarified butter (ghee)

Heat the oil in a pan and fry the onion and roughly chopped carrot. Add the roasted bones and tendons. Fry for 10 minutes, then add the wine, stock, and herbs. Chop the juniper berries a little to release the flavor. Simmer the sauce for 2.5 hours, then drain through a sieve and reduce on low heat for an hour, to obtain a smooth texture.
In another pan, sear the meat in butter, 4 minutes on each side, basting with the juices from the pan. The meat should still be pink in the center. When cooked, allow to rest in a warm place for 10 minutes, so the juices settle.

½ cup (100 ml) oil
1 onion
1 carrot, roughly chopped
Bones from the venison back
1 cup (200 ml) Merlot
1½ cups (300 ml) beef stock
1 bay leaf
1 sprig of thyme
20 juniper berries

TARRAGON ŠTRUKELJ
(DOUGH ROLL):
Combine the flour, yolk, oil, vinegar, and water and knead until the dough is smooth. Allow to rest in the fridge for half an hour.

4½ ounces (125 g) cake flour
1 egg yolk
½ tablespoon sunflower oil
1 teaspoon apple cider vinegar
⅓ cup (85 ml) water

For the filling, mash the cottage cheese, add the sour cream, egg, chopped tarragon, and salt, and stir well. Melt the butter in a saucepan.
Roll out the dough on a cloth as thin as possible. Spread it with the melted butter and then with the cottage cheese filling, covering three-quarters of the surface. Using the cloth, roll into a štrukelj, starting on the side with the filling.
Scatter the breadcrumbs over a clean damp cloth, place the štrukelj on top, then wrap it and tie the cloth at the ends. Cook in boiling water for 20 minutes.

10½ ounces (300 g) cottage cheese
½ cup (100 ml) sour cream
1 egg
1¾ ounces (50 g) tarragon leaves, chopped
Salt
2 ounces (60 g) butter
3 tablespoons (40 g) breadcrumbs

CRANBERRIES:
Wash the cranberries and combine with the sugar and lemon juice in a saucepan. Cook for 45 minutes, then cool to obtain a thick jam.

¾ pound (400 g) fresh cranberries
½ cup (100 g) sugar
Juice of ½ lemon

Peel and chop the vegetables, blanch quickly in salted water, and sauté in melted butter. Briefly fry the breadcrumbs in butter.

2½ ounces (70 g) rutabaga
1¾ ounces (50 g) celeriac
1¾ ounces (50 g) red Swiss chard (stems only)
1 ounce (30 g) butter
Salt

TO SERVE:
Pour some meat sauce onto a plate. Slice the meat, place onto the sauce, and season with fleur de sel. Add slices of štrukelj and pour the crumbs and butter over the top. Add the sautéed vegetables and cranberry jam.

PRIMOŽ KRIŠELJ,
PRI ŠUŠTARJU ECO FARM.
BLACKSTRAP PIGS.

BLACKSTRAP PIGS

Fat is good. That's not something you would have heard, say, ten years ago, especially not from the mouths of Americans who eschewed fat but did not seem shy about sugars, and then wondered why they were still getting fat. But the latest research tells us that, as long as you don't suffer from any particular condition, butter is better for you than margarine and good kinds of fats are good for you. All in moderation, of course, and it can be hard to be moderate when fat tastes so damn good. While there are still concerns about carcinogens in the most beloved of all fatty meats—I'm looking at you, bacon, a meat product so universally beloved that it even appeared as a topping on ice cream served at McDonald's—fatty cuts of meat are the ones with the most flavor. Rendering the fat or even processing and consuming it directly as a spread is not the death trap that it was once considered. Though if you've got to go, death by bacon consumption sounds about as good a way as any.

The pure milk-white fat from healthy pigs, affectionately known as lard (*mast* in Slovene), is an absolutely delicious thing when spread on bread directly or used for cooking. Sautéed with oil, cracklings add bursts of salty, luscious, smoky, umami, porky flavor to anything cooked in them (if you think you might not be a fan of Brussels sprouts, try them sautéed in *ocvirki*, cracklings). And there are certain pigs that produce more and better fat than others. Those breeds are the ones most prized by those in the know, like JB.

Butchers like to joke about the public's obsession with lean meat. Lean meat can still taste good, but it is not the most desirable for true foodies, and too little fat means a dryer piece of meat with less flavor. That's just the way it is. The key is to educate people not to be afraid of fat, but to know how to use it and to know which kinds of fats are the good ones.

Which explains why I am standing ankle deep in mud in a forest in Hotemaže, in the mountainous Gorenjska region, at the eco farm Pri Šuštarju, run by Primož and Polona Krišelj. Before me snort, wink, and affectionately wallow two very special breeds of pig. One of them could easily be mistaken at a distance for a bear or a sheep, as it's covered in a coarse white curly fur. This breed is indigenous to Slovenia and adjacent Hungary and is called Mangalica. If ever there was a pig that would look at home in the company of cavemen, this is it. A black and probing snout and dark set eyes are surrounded by a shaggy mane of bristly off-white fur, like some inflated pipe cleaner on four chunky legs.

The other breed, indigenous only to the territory that is now Slovenia, is called *Krško polje* pig, or Blackstrap. Blackstrap are of similar hefty girth but are known and named for their white skin with a thick black stripe that runs around it. These two breeds have unusually high fat content that is unusually delicious and so are most prized by in-the-know fat-seeking cooks and high-end chefs. JB is in good company, as Primož and Polona provide pigs to many of the country's top restaurants.

Primož is a large man with eyes streaked with crow's feet and kindness. He came rather late to farming, having taught and met his wife when they were both teachers at the agricultural secondary school. On his farm he raises chickens, these two breeds of pigs, and keeps around 300 sheep of another special indigenous variety, Jezerska-Solčavska, named after a gorgeous mountain lake, Jezersko, that is just a couple miles from his farm. It doesn't get any more local than raising an indigenous breed of sheep that is not only specific to your country but specific to a few kilometers from your house.

His passion for details and love of animals is such that he prefers to give sheep the millennia-old exercise of walking them up to the mountain pasture, where he lets them graze. While most sheep farmers pack their stock into trucks and drive them to pasture, he and a few colleagues and dogs laboriously march alongside them, a good six hours uphill, to bring them there. Several times a week. This is not just a six-hour stroll, but strenuous uphill hiking, punctuated by frequent sprints on awkward terrain to cut off sheep trying to make a break for it. It's the stuff of Slovenian idyll, as the legendary shepherd boy, Kekec, the most beloved children's folk hero and focus of three classic films, was a young shepherd in similarly idyllic mountain pastures. With his love of nature, bright smile, and wily eyes, Primož could pass for a grownup Kekec.

But the focus today is down in the forest at the edge of Primož's fields, where the ground has been churned to mud by exceedingly heavy cloven hooves and charmingly expressive snouts.

JB assures me that cutlets and chops from these pigs are amazing, but what he's after are the cuts and preparations that focus on that gorgeous white fat. This means bacon (*slanina*), its close cousin pancetta (*pančeta*), lard (*mast*), cracklings (*ocvirki*), and those chunky legs that will end up as the finest *pršut*, prosciutto, when sent to the likes of Uroš Klinec, hero of a previous chapter.

Primož eats only meat from animals raised on his own farm but exhibits an interesting and endearing dynamic when discussing it, one I've found in other meaty protagonists of this book. While he is wise enough not to consider the animals he raises as pets, as that would make his job too emotionally difficult, he cannot bring himself to kill or butcher them himself and finds it genuinely difficult to hand them off to those who do. A misty look, and what could be mistaken for tears, comes to his eyes when he talks about it.

We all want to eat meat. Well, everyone except for vegetarians. But almost no one wants to think about where it comes from. This is, of course, hypocritical, but it is also an understandable defense mechanism and it is very human, if not humane. I am an enthusiastic carnivore, but I would find it upsetting to be present when an animal is killed, even if I will happily dive into the resulting cutlets and sausages. I am reconciled to that hypocrisy, but if I think too much about it, my morality gets tied into knots. So, like most of us, I tend to push it to the side. Not to think about it, if at all possible. Primož is confronted with this on a weekly basis, and functions well, but is unable to hide from it the way most of us are.

He sublimates this conflict into making the best life possible for his animals, so they have a good run, and he puts a lot of love into caring for them. The result is happy creatures and what any chef will tell you are the finest pork products that one can find, bar none. The late Anthony Bourdain would've loved it here.

After a photo shoot in which the pigs seemed more delighted to be photographed than Primož, his wife Polona lays out an incredible spread on the rough-cut wooden table on the covered patio beside their beautiful wood-beamed house, which looks like the sort of high-end ski chalet that one might find in Vail, Colorado, and which is very exotic around these parts, in a country largely covered with perfectly fine but generic breeze block houses of cookie cutter shapes and sizes. Their enormous dog, Šaja, looks strikingly similar to a canine version of a Mangalica pig, with a luxurious deep-pile coat that acts as soft armor, as this breed was long raised throughout the Alps to help shepherds fend off attacks from bears and wolves.

On the table, we find a wide variety of pork products, and I wonder if I've dozed off and woken in porcine heaven. *Zaseka*, a spread made of lard and smoked pork bits. *Ocvirki*, knuckle-sized cracklings that look like Cracker Jacks and result in the world's best fried eggs (or Brussels sprouts, or anything, for that matter) when used instead of butter or oil to sauté them. They also stud some killer mashed potatoes. *Špeh*, that unctuous bone-colored lard with meaty streaks is sliced paper thin, so it quite literally melts when placed on the tongue. There was *pršut* sliced thin off the leg, with the fatty portion still glazed onto the meat, along with pancetta and bacon, smoked and unsmoked.

I am amazed by the variety of flavors, textures, and wonders that can emerge from a single beast. This is not only in terms of quantity, but in diversity. From fresh to smoked to air-dried, every part of the pig is used. JB is particularly fond of bits that you wouldn't necessarily think of to eat, especially not as high-end cuisine. Witness his remarkably fresh-tasting terrine, almost salad-like in its lightness and tartness, which is based on pig's ears.

Satiated with pork and a fine young white wine bearing a label on which we see a photograph of Primož superimposed onto the body of young shepherd boy, Kekec, I lean back and admire the nearby view of the Alps. When I die, this is what I might imagine heaven is like. I wonder what sort of heaven pigs dream of? Very likely something akin to this mud-churned forest overseen by a man of great care and kindness like Primož.

EGG YOLKS AND CRACKLINGS WITH PARSLEY ROOT AND LOVAGE PURÉES

CRACKLINGS:

Dice the lard into ½-inch cubes. Pour just enough water into a saucepan to cover the base and add the lard. Place on low heat, add the half onion without cutting it, season with salt, and stir. Continue stirring as the lard melts, until you are left with melted fat and cracklings. When the onion is golden, remove from heat and cool the cracklings.

7 ounces (200 g) raw meaty back lard of Mangalica pork
½ onion
1 tablespoon (10 g) salt, halved

PARSLEY ROOT:

Wash the parsley roots and cut them into chunks. Pour just enough water into a pressure cooker to cover the base, add the parsley roots, salt, and baking soda, cover, and cook for 15 minutes. Drain the parsley roots and press them through a fine sieve to get a smooth purée, without the water in which they were cooked.

3 ounces (80 g) parsley root
Pinch of baking soda

SPINACH AND LOVAGE:

Blanch the greens in boiling water for 4 minutes, then drain and place into a bowl with iced water. When the greens are cold, drain well and chop them.
Melt the butter in a saucepan and add the greens. Braise for 10 minutes, then blend and pass through a fine sieve to make a smooth purée.

1 ounce (30 g) lovage
1 ounce (30 g) spinach
3½ ounces (100 g) butter

TO SERVE:

Arrange both purées on a plate, carefully add a raw egg yolk and some microgreens for decoration, and finally top with hot cracklings.

4 egg yolks
Microgreens, salt

PIG EAR TERRINE,
RED CABBAGE SALAD,
SUNFLOWER OIL MARINADE,
AND FRIED BUCKWHEAT

———————

Soak the buckwheat for an hour, drain, add fresh water and some salt and cook it for 25 minutes. Drain, spread out on a tray, and dry at room temperature for a day.

3 ounces (80 g) buckwheat groats
½ cup (100 ml) oil for deep-frying

Wash the pig ears, place in a pot, and cover with water. Add the roughly chopped vegetables, salt, and herbs, cover the pot, and simmer for two and a half hours on low heat. When the pig ears are cooked, remove them (and the bay leaf) and reserve the remaining liquid. Remove the large piece of cartilage at the base of each ear. Layer the warm ears in a mold lined with cling film, first covering the entire base and continuing to layer until all the ears are used. Cover with another piece of cling film and weigh down the layers so they are well-compressed. Leave in the fridge overnight, then remove from the mold.

2¼ pounds (1 kg) pig ears
1 onion, roughly chopped
1 carrot, roughly chopped
½ celeriac, roughly chopped
1 bay leaf
1 sprig parsley
Salt, black peppercorns

MARINADE:
Place the egg, the cooled liquid in which the ears were cooked, vinegar, salt, pepper, and mustard into a bowl and blend with an immersion blender. Slowly add the sunflower oil and continue blending to obtain an emulsion.

1 egg
½ cup (100 ml) cooled liquid, left over from cooking the pig's ears
1 tablespoon apple cider vinegar
Pinch of salt and pepper
1 teaspoon mustard
½ cup (100 ml) sunflower oil

Quickly deep-fry the buckwheat in oil at 350°F (175°C), so that it pops.

CABBAGE:
Thin slice the cabbage and season with salt, vinegar, and oil for a crunchy salad.

8½ ounces (240 g) red cabbage
Salt
1⅓ tablespoons (20 ml) apple cider vinegar
¼ cup (50 ml) sunflower oil

TO SERVE:
Using a meat slicer or mandoline, slice the terrine thin and arrange on a plate. Add some mustard seeds, gravy, and marinade, and finally the popped buckwheat and cabbage salad.

1¾ ounces (50 g) mustard seeds
½ cup (100 ml) roast pork gravy

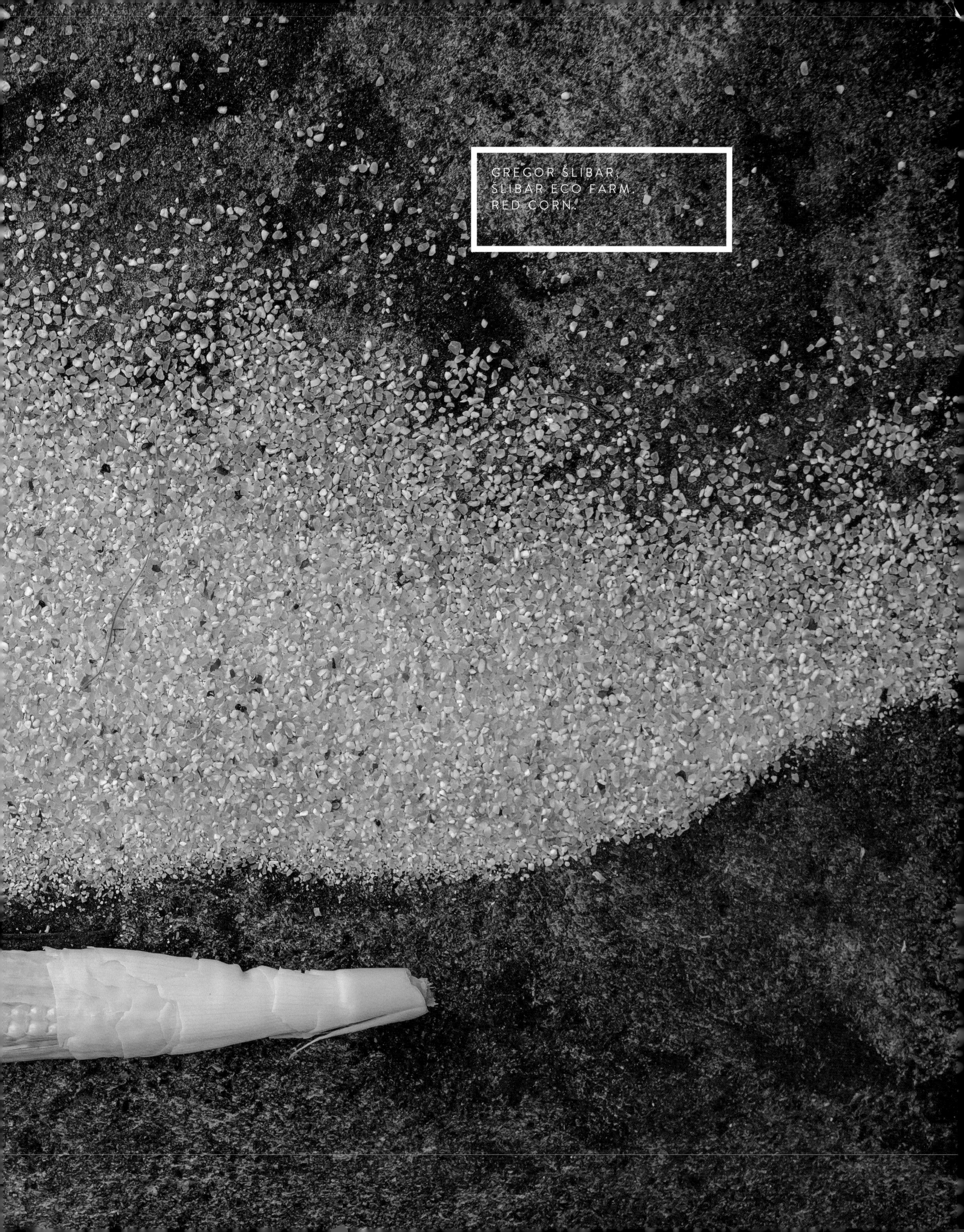

GREGOR ŠLIBAR,
ŠLIBAR ECO FARM.
RED CORN.

RED CORN

The farm is perched on a plateau overlooking the medieval town of Tržič, with the Alps spiking up in the near distance. It's like the scenography for a Surrealist play: How could such precipitous and picturesque mountains be so near? How can so elaborate a farm be just a stone's throw away from the cobbled center of a town? And how can the proprietor possibly get so much work done, and of such high quality, with his six beautiful little children running about, weaving around sacks of grain, darting between their father's legs, motoring in a mechanical toy car in which an eight-year-old daughter sits and "drives" her three-year-old brother in slow, whirring loops around the stone courtyard? It's a working farm, but not the sort that I would expect.

The Šlibar family farm is one of the most gracious and elegant in the country. A row of "glamping" wooden cottages, each hand-built by Gregor, the father of the family, are available for tourists, and they are regularly full throughout the summer. But some of these cottages house agriculture students from around the world, who travel here to experience life working on an organic farm as part of a work-study experience, what's called WWOOFing (World Wide Organization of Organic Farmers). The day that I arrive with JB and Matjaž, an American and a British agriculture student are tending to the cabbage patch, while a French and a Portuguese student prepare grain for stone-grinding. The Šlibars not only have six children of their own but host countless working houseguests. Evening meals are elaborate banquets, with the table often set for twelve. I'm assured that Mrs. Šlibar's cooking is the highlight of the stay, and I don't doubt it. From the look of the produce in their small on-site shop, and from what JB tells me about the quality of all they make, this sounds like as good a place as the planet has to offer to try your hand at farming, whether as a casual agritourism-style guest, or as a work-study agriculture student here for months at a time.

What drew JB first to the Šlibar farm was Gregor's flexibility. Most farms grind corn into polenta in one way, the way they think is "right," and do so in such quantities, on a sort of automatic pilot, that even chefs like JB, a household name in Slovenia, are obliged to take their product or leave it. Not Gregor. He worked directly with JB, experimenting with the coarseness of the grind, until the chef was perfectly satisfied. This required JB cooking batch after batch of polenta, all with the same corn, mind you, but in quest for the perfect consistency, texture, and mouthfeel. The willingness to remain a boutique operation, even when the Šlibars easily sell out of all the products they produce—grains and flour, of course, but also dried and fresh fruit, like pears that dehydrate into tiny grenades of flavor, apple juice, apple cider vinegar, home-baked breads, jams with 100 percent fruit content, and even Slovenia's first bio beers—is a sign of passion for quality and personal service that is rare to find.

Matjaž scouts locations for the photoshoot. It's all so preposterously picturesque, not like a Disney version of a farm, but a real, working, gritty farm with rusted pieces of machinery that sit like fossils against an elegantly patchy barn wall, the sort of dilapidated look that city-folk pay extra for ("distressed" Restoration Hardware–style). A grain silo, where the grinding takes place, could be the stage set for a horror film, all vaulting gothic darkness, but for the warm and dust-dappled streak of sunlight slicing through a hole in the roof, and the rich smell of fresh-crushed buckwheat.

While Slovenia is particularly known for buckwheat, a dietary staple promoted abroad when it was included as a key ingredient in Slovenia Vodka (made famous by the celebrity of one of its investors, actor Bill Murray), JB has brought me to the Šlibar farm for polenta made from a very particular, indigenous type of corn.

A red corn. *Trdinka* is the name of the corn, and while it comes in white and yellow varieties, it is the red version (*rdeča trdinka*) that steals the headlines. We pull over in the Šlibar's field. Row upon row of stalks, all about as high as an elephant's eye, but with a surreal touch: the silky "hair" that puffs out of the corn husks is, indeed, tinted pink. It looks like some sort of sea creature, or possibly a sign of End Times, when the corn begins to bleed. Reddish-pink tufts are scattered among the long, green stalks and the kernels are likewise shaded pink. When ground for polenta, the yellow meal is dotted with red flecks, like incarnadine stars in a sundrenched night sky.

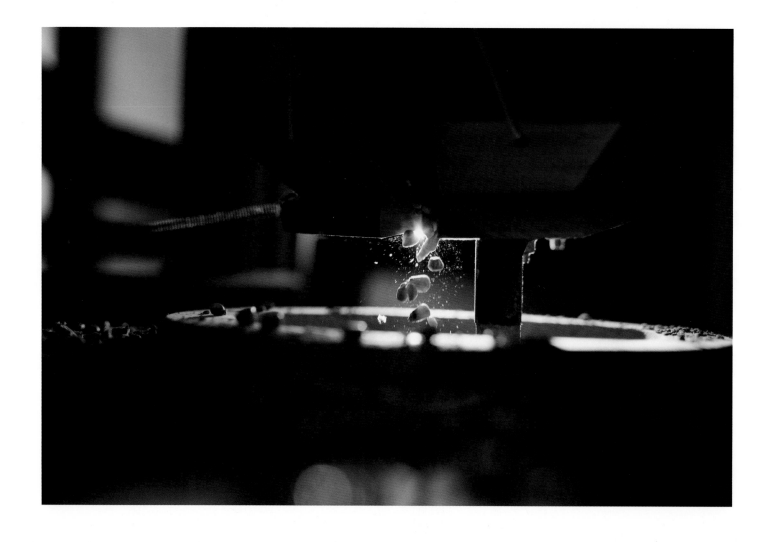

JB loves *trdinka* because it is "ours," by which he means that it is indigenous to Slovenia. The taste is delicate and he sources from Gregor, because Gregor will make boutique grinds on his stone mill, perfectly gauged to allow JB to make his magical polenta back at the restaurant. JB also clearly has great affection for Gregor, and Gregor, in turn, is visibly proud to be the chosen provider for a chef he so admires. This is no mere business relationship, either. The two have been friendly for so long that JB has watched Gregor's six children grow, all running around the stone-paved courtyard and its snowfall of spilled flour and stray grains that have not yet been swept up.

We pause for a photoshoot. I assume that Matjaž will seat us in front of one of those calendar-picturesque barn walls, or perhaps with the steepled and gabled townscape of Tržič in the middle distance. But no, he opts for the atmospheric shadow of the pig sty. I wouldn't normally object, but it seems that the resident flies think that Christmas has come early, and we are swarmed and crawled upon, as we wait for the light to fall just so on our faces, achieving the chiaroscuro effect that Matjaž is after. I've been on more comfortable photoshoots, but few as atmospheric.

Gregor and his wife are waiting outside the sty, with homemade schnapps to taste (and bring home—Matjaž brought a bottle back to China, where he lives most of the year, a true taste of the Slovenian countryside), fresh bread in thick slices, and bottles of the homemade bio beer. Before we set off for home, I'm sure to get Gregor's number, as I plan to book an overnight at one of his glamping guest cottages—my young daughters would love to play farmer on this postcard-perfect working boutique farm, nestled at the foot of the Alps, with its Alice in Wonderland red-haired corn on show.

This is the part of Slovenia where I live, between Ljubljana, a 30-minute-drive away, and the steepest Alpine peaks half an hour to the North. It is the region with significant Germanic influences, where grannies speak Slovene, Serbo-Croatian, and German, and call a plate a *talar*, from German *der Teller*. A classic lunch is a pair of sausages on a pile of sauerkraut or sour turnip, both dressed with plenty of cracklings. In this country friendship—and even kindness—needs to be earned. But once you have made friends here, they are your friends for life. Most Slovenes will tell you that they only have a few friends. For friendly acquaintances, those you go out with for drinks, but don't share personal stuff, they use another word—*kolega*. This is more than a "colleague" in English. So I was honored when Gregor gave me a hug after the visit and invited me to come back with my family. The day we had spent together and our common friend, JB, meant that I was more than *kolega*. Working hard all day with red corn, a glass or two of homemade schnapps before lunch, and avoiding a fly attack during a photoshoot contribute greatly to making friends.

Back at the restaurant kitchen, JB carves gently wobbly blocks of baked polenta. He'll use *rdeča trdinka* to make the creamy variety, too, but he has plans for a firmer version for a recipe that is designed for ease of home cooking: blocks of polenta, flecked with a constellation of red specks, topped with a luxurious sauce and finished with edible flowers that he brought from his home garden.

He asks me if I know how to work an espresso machine. I say yes, but as he sends me out to fire up some coffee for us, I realize that he means that gorgeous, very expensive espresso machine behind the restaurant bar, studded with retro-looking mechanical dials and with a Ferrari aesthetic. My confidence wanes, but I give it a shot. It takes me an embarrassingly long time to figure out the coffee grinder (turns out it has a button-less touch feature to start grinding, but then you have to touch it again for it to stop grinding). Looks like I'll also have my first experience frantically sweeping up fresh-ground coffee from the bar floor. Then, while I can untwist the handle of the espresso machine into which the grounds are packed, I can't seem to get it to twist back into place. This results in half of my coffee spraying laterally, instead of into the espresso cup beneath. I don't think I'll be replacing any of JB's bar staff anytime soon.

As the first dish for this book shot by our food photographer, Manca (and this being my first experience with a cookbook), I was fascinated not only to see JB at work, but to see how Manca composes the photographs. JB is inventing the dish as he goes, at least its presentation, and there's a friendly dialogue with Manca, JB regularly asking for her thoughts. One of his attributes that I admire is his down-to-earth willingness to engage the opinions of others. He may be an artist, but he's without pretense.

Manca has a small arsenal of beautiful, homemade flatware onto which each dish can be arranged: burnt umber ceramics, slate squares, black-baked porcelain, rough-cut stone bowls, even a plate made of concrete. She prefers to photograph with only natural light, setting up on the terrace behind the restaurant. JB rummages through his car, parked out back, and emerges, smiling. In his hand, like a knight bearing a lance, he carries a full-length corn stalk, cut from the Šlibar's field. Back in the kitchen, three hot loaves of corn-based bread emerge from the oven. They all look good to me, but JB smells each deeply, flips them over, and taps the base, trying to determine the prime example.

While he floats around his kitchen, more at home here than he is at his home, he offers some useful tips for handling corn. I recall a quote from Garrison Keillor, the great American humorist and radio personality: "People have tried and tried," he said, "but sex is not better than sweet corn." While Europeans eat their share of corn, it is primarily in the form of polenta, with some cultures—I'm looking at you, France—considering unprocessed corn as food fit only for pigs. Lucky pigs.

Sweet corn, on the cob and just lightly boiled, is one of the great, simple culinary pleasures. But home cooks often employ a more complicating approach than is strictly necessary. First of all, there's no need to strip the husk to see if the corn is healthy. A simple squeeze along its length will reveal whether worms or rot are present. When it comes to boiling, it's actually a better way forward to strip away only the most fibrous and hard outer husks, but leave a single layer of green "skin" around the corn when you pop it into the boiling water. This retains more flavor and, when you pull the corn out, the husk keeps it nice and warm until it's ready to be eaten.

Slovenes like JB grew up eating corn in its non-polenta state primarily when on holiday on the Dalmatian coast—the preferred summer destination for the majority of the population of Yugoslavia (state-run firms usually offered workers a week's paid vacation at resorts in Dalmatia as a standard right). There, grilled corn is a regular seaside treat, with cobs wrapped in foil until purchased. Sweet corn is full of natural sugars that begin to turn into starch as soon as the ear is picked. Corn should be cooked very briefly. The longer it cooks, the tougher it gets, so JB suggests that 30 seconds is ideal. The boiling water should never be salted, as this also results in toughness. But once the corn is ready to eat, a dusting of salt and a lather of butter is all that's needed.

Despite all complications that top chefs like to introduce, JB appreciates raw ingredients—literally. Wherever we go, he sniffs the fields, picks herbs, and tells me to eat them. Where I see a meadow in need of some mowing, he sees lunch. The same with grains, the famous Slovene buckwheat, this unique, unworldly variety of corn. Complicated things can be good, but simple things can be good as well. A great master is aware of that and only introduces complications if they can offer something new. But naturally, one needs raw ingredients as fine as these, if you want to get away with something that simple.

BUCKWHEAT BREAD WITH KRŠKO POLJE LARD SPREAD, ROAST GARLIC, RADISH, AND DEEP-FRIED BUCKWHEAT GROATS

───────

BREAD:

Combine buckwheat flour and white flour in a bowl, then add crumbled yeast and water. Knead well, transfer to the work surface, add the walnuts and a pinch of salt, then knead again to distribute them throughout the dough. Place the dough in a bowl, cover with cling film, and leave to rise.

After an hour, add another pinch of salt, knead again, and leave to rise a second time for half an hour or until it doubles in size. Heat oven to 360°F (180°C).

Brush the loaf with milk, place in the oven, and bake for half an hour with the steam setting on. If your oven does not have steam function, place a shallow dish with some water on the bottom of the oven. After half an hour increase the temperature to 375°F (190°C) and bake for a further 40 minutes without the steam setting. When baked, remove the bread from the oven and leave to cool.

7 ounces (200 g) buckwheat flour
10½ ounces (300 g) all-purpose flour
About ½ ounce (12 g) fresh yeast
1 cup (200 ml) water
3½ ounces (100 g) walnut halves, roughly chopped
Salt
¼ cup (50 ml) milk to glaze

BUCKWHEAT GROATS:

Pour the buckwheat groats into salted boiling water, stir, and cook for 10 minutes, until the grains split open. Drain the groats, spread them on a piece of baking paper, and dehydrate in a convection oven for 6 hours at 140°F (60°C). If the grains stick together, they can be separated when dry by lightly rubbing them between the hands. Quickly deep-fry the dry groats in oil at 340°F (170°C), so that the grains pop. Drain on kitchen paper.

3½ ounces (100 g) buckwheat groats
Salt
2½ cups (500 ml) oil for deep frying

LARD SPREAD:

Cut the lard into chunks and cook for an hour with the vegetables and herbs in a small amount of water. When the lard is cooked, drain and grind it in a meat grinder together with the cooked onion and garlic (discard the rest of the vegetables and spices). Add salt to taste. If the mixture is too thick, add a splash cooking water. Mix well and leave to cool until you get a spreadable paste.

1 pound + 2 ounces (500 g) piece Krško polje (Blackstrap) raw pork lard from the belly
2 cloves garlic
1 onion
1 carrot
½ celeriac
1½ tablespoons (20 g) salt
Black peppercorns to taste
1 bay leaf

ROAST GARLIC:

Cut the garlic head in half horizontally and brush the cut sides with butter. Sprinkle with some salt and roast in a convection oven for half an hour at 340°F (170°C).

2 heads garlic
1 ounce (30 g) butter
Pinch of salt

TO SERVE:

Cut the bread into thick slices, spread them with lard spread, sprinkle with the fried buckwheat groats, and top with the baked garlic, thinly sliced radishes, and radish seed pods.

3½ ounces (100 g) radishes
3½ tablespoons (50 g) radish seed pods

SOFT RED POLENTA WITH CHANTERELLE SAUCE AND SOUR CREAM

SOFT POLENTA:

Boil the water with butter and salt, add the polenta, and cook for 1 hour, stirring constantly. If it is too thick, add a little more water and continue cooking.

4¼ cups (1 L) water
3 tablespoons (40 g) butter
1 tablespoon (10 g) salt
7 ounces (200 g) red polenta
(made from "trdinka" corn)

FRIED POLENTA:

Melt the butter and sprinkle in the polenta. Fry slowly on low heat for half an hour, stirring, so that it becomes crispy.

3 tablespoons (40 g) butter
3½ tablespoons (50 g) red polenta

POLENTA CHIPS:

Spread a thin layer of the cooked polenta on a silicone tray and dehydrate in the oven at 130°F (55°C) for 10 hours. When dry, break it into pieces and quickly deep-fry in oil at 350°F (175°C) to get chips.

CHANTERELLE SAUCE:

Wash the chanterelles and cut them into pieces. Chop the onion and fry it in butter until golden, then add chanterelles, frying a further 5 minutes. Season with salt and pepper and add stock. Simmer a few more minutes until the sauce thickens.
Whisk the sour cream until it is smooth.

9 ounces (250 g) chanterelles
1 onion
4¾ tablespoons (60 g) butter
Salt and pepper
½ cup (100 ml) beef stock
½ cup (100 ml) sour cream
Wood sorrel for decoration and taste

TO SERVE:

Spoon the soft polenta in a bowl. Top with chanterelle sauce and place a spoonful of sour cream in the center. Garnish with fried polenta, polenta chips, and a little wood sorrel for freshness.

DAMJAN ŠTEMBERGER.
LAMB.

LAMB

I'll get to why I am hiding in the car with the doors locked in a minute. We are perched upon a mountain that took half an hour to drive up. Twilight grips the sky and it is a race for Matjaž to snap our subject, Damjan Štemberger, before darkness enfolds us. Twilight is not the camera's best friend, especially when we're not using a tripod, so we keep the pickup truck's headlights on. This casts a horror movie glow around Damjan. And he fits the part. Damjan is a mountain of a man, absolutely enormous. Not fat, but big, colossal, like a former center for the Denver Broncos or The Mountain from *Game of Thrones*, minus the beard. In the chiaroscuro half-light up here, between the headlights and twilight and night pushing down, it is pretty creepy, but that's not the real reason that this feels like I'm in an outtake from a horror movie. That would be the mutilated sheep corpse that we came across the moment we stepped out of the pickup. It had been so freshly rent to shreds that there was still steam rising from it.

On the drive up, Damjan told of the trouble he has keeping his thousand sheep safe from bears and wolves while they are all alone here, all night, atop the mountain. He has tried 6-foot-tall (1.8 meter) electrified fences, but wolves managed to dig a tunnel underneath them. He set up perimeter alarms, but it takes so long for anyone to reach the grazing pastures on the mountaintop that they would inevitably arrive too late. He kept a pack of bear-fighting dogs, but they would gradually disappear, too. Those that did remain started to side with the enemy: they underwent a shift after exposure to the sheep's blood over the course of various skirmishes with wolves and bears, in which sheep would be hurt and some killed before the dogs chased away the predators. After a few years, these dogs would start to turn on the sheep they were bred to protect, developing a taste for them.

So, there is not much that can be done, and the steaming, quartered corpse which has been dragged outside the electrified fence reminds me a little of a scene from *Jurassic Park*. It also means that the bear responsible for this is not far away and has an unfinished meal right next to where we are trying to have a nice little photoshoot. I'm no zoologist, but something tells me this is not the best idea. Hence my camping out inside the pickup truck, while JB smokes outside and keeps an eye on the darkening forest a few hundred meters from where we stand.

JB describes Damjan as one of the hardest-working people he knows, and I can see why when he begins to describe his work routine. He began his career selling porcini mushrooms. In his first year, he was pleased to sell around 220 pounds (100 kg) during the season, selling 2¼ or 4½ pounds (1 or 2 kg) here or there, to various restaurants like JB's. In his second year, he had escalated his business to selling a ton (2,000 pounds) in one season, and now he sells around 100 tons (200,000 pounds) a year. But it's not just porcini mushrooms. He sells all sorts of what he calls "forest fruits," including 70 tons (140,000 pounds) of blueberries, and a similar quantity of strawberries, chanterelles, and much more every year. He is one of the biggest farmers (physically and professionally) in the region, selling to Austria and Italy and Hungary and Croatia and relying on a small army of foragers who bring him fresh produce every day when in season, for him to sell on to high-end restaurants and farmers' markets. His prime season for foraged forest goods is between two to four months long, depending on the caprices of the weather, so he is working up to twenty-hour days when he can, to compensate for the lean months. Most evenings during the season he will set off at 8 or 9 o'clock at night to deliver to Croatian customers. That's at least an hour drive each way, and it is often just the start of his night's work, which comes after a long day, as well. His success is hard-won. His phone is constantly ringing, and he explains that he is not able to turn it off, because customers will call with a need for a certain type of produce within a few hours. Consider, for example, an order for 4½ pounds (2 kg) of porcini mushrooms for lunch. If he gets the call at five in the morning and he doesn't take it, or if he delivers the goods too late, he misses the lunch rush and the restaurant no longer needs the mushrooms and they will go to one of his competitors next time.

There's an element of luck and a heavy dose of tactical thinking in his business. Damjan explains that there may be months where he makes almost nothing, but he can also make as much as $60,000 in a single month—an enormous amount, when one considers that a solid Slovenian salary is about $1,220 a month. But he has also lost up to $18,000 in a single day, when once he ordered 3 tons (6,000 pounds) of fresh porcini and, due to traffic and a breakdown, they remained too long inside the hot truck, and they were spoiled by the time they reached their destination.

Emotion flashes in his eyes when he talks about the need to work hard to support his family and to pay his staff. A real man takes care of his family and those who rely on him, and Damjan is well aware of this. He pays the price by sleeping as little as two hours a night during high season.

I am told that Bosnians are by far the world's best shepherds, sheep whisperers, a comment I have heard from many people and not just from this region (they are apparently also goat whisperers, as Aleš Winkler hires only Bosnians to tend to his flock). Damjan employs five full-time shepherds to watch over his thousand sheep, as part of an extensive staff. He also seems to own most of the town surroundings of Ilirska Bistrica, which is where his pastures can be found.

Sheep are Damjan's passion and they calm the sea within him. He describes his delight in coming to the mountaintop a couple of times a season, bringing a few bags of stale bread and calling out to the sheep. They might be a few kilometers away, but they scamper towards him. It is particularly charming to see so mighty a man grow soft and smile, relating how it delights him when they eat out of his hand.

The indigenous breed of sheep raised by Damjan is called Jezersko-Solčava, a complicated nomenclature that refers to two northern mountain regions, around Jezersko (a mountain lake very close to the farm of Primož Krišelj, who keeps these sheep in addition to his Blackstrap pigs) and Solčava, a valley near the Austria-Slovenia border. The sheep are prized for both meat and wool, with strong legs to navigate mountain terrain. They are low in fat, which tends to be a plus for lamb meat (whereas fat is preferable in pork). They also produce a good yield of around 11 pounds (5 kg) of wool per year. This breed is recognizable by tear-shaped black patterns, sometimes described as "eyeglasses," around the eyes. I see in Damjan the same gentle tug of war within him that I saw in Primož and his pigs. These are farmers who respect, admire, care for, and even love their animals. They know that the animals are raised for food, but are determined to give them the best life they can, to defend them and treat them appropriately.

Satisfied with the photographs taken, and the fact that we were not mauled by a bear in the process of taking said photographs, we get back in the pickup truck and head down the mountain. Matjaž, JB, and me are all tired, but Damjan is so delighted that we are here that he wants to show us more of his holdings.

He takes us down the mountain to see his headquarters, which is shining and spotless in a way that I could never imagine for a location that processes organic material full-time. A warehouse that you can back a truck into is ready for shipments of berries and figs and all manner of mushrooms, which are stacked far above my head height in refrigerated rooms. Here we find the scale and expensive gadgetry of a proper factory, but it must be kept in mind that most of his products are foraged by hand, and so this mass of deliciousness represents the time and gathering efforts of hundreds of people over hundreds of miles, who bring the best ingredients to him so he can distribute them.

A portion of his headquarters is dedicated to butchering the sheep, and it looks like an operating theater. Hospital-clean, he is scrupulous about cleanliness and professionalism and keeping the sheep as happy as sheep can be prior to the big moment. He normally sells whole sheep, sending perhaps one a week to JB, but he has a particularly enthusiastic Chinese restaurant that takes 15 whole sheep a week.

It's past midnight and we are dozing off in our shoes, but Damjan's night will go on. Sensing our fatigue, he wraps up the tour, but not before he loads our trunk with wooden crates of fresh figs and red currants and raspberries . . . and not before taking us out for the only midnight snack available in the town of Ilirska Bistrica—a kebab. Not being exactly the freshest Jezersko-Solčava lamb meat, JB politely claims not to be hungry, but Matjaž and I enthusiastically gorge. There's a time and a place for the finest lamb available on the planet, and midnight in a greasy kebab joint ain't it. Sometimes a generic kebab is all you really need. But given my druthers, I'll take Damjan's lamb, as prepared by JB. Now, why didn't I think to ask JB to get behind the kebab stand counter and fire up a gourmet version for us?

SLOW-ROAST LAMB WITH THYME SAUCE, SAUTÉED POTATOES, ROAST JERUSALEM ARTICHOKES, AND DEEP-FRIED SAGE

Season the lamb with salt, place on a baking tray, and add the thyme and bay leaf. Roughly chop the onion and carrot and add the vegetables into the tray. Add the stock and roast in the oven on the half-steam setting for 2 hours at 230°F (110°C). Then change the oven function to dry heat and roast a further 45 minutes at 250°F (120°C), and then 30 minutes at 320°F (160°C). Baste the meat frequently with the tray juices. If your oven does not have a steam function, place a shallow dish with some water in it at the bottom of the oven.

2¼ pounds (1 kg) lamb shoulder, bone-in
Thyme
1 bay leaf
1 onion
1 carrot
1 cup (200 ml) stock
3½ ounces (100 g) pork caul fat
Herbs for wrapping (parsley, rosemary, mint, thyme, edible flowers, salt)
3½ tablespoons (50 g) clarified butter (ghee)

Remove the roast meat from the bones and transfer it into a smaller tray so that you get about a 1½-inch layer of meat. Weigh down the meat and chill in the fridge.

Arrange the herbs and flowers on the caul fat. Cut the cooled meat into 1½ × 1½ × 4-inch rectangles and wrap in the caul fat. Sautée in butter in a frying pan on low heat.

Strain the sauce from the baking tray, add a sprig of thyme, and reduce slightly to thicken.

Boil the unpeeled potatoes in salted water until soft. Peel the cooked potatoes and cut into thin slices.
Heat the lard in a saucepan and fry the thinly sliced onion until golden brown. Add the potato, season with salt and pepper, and fry another 5 minutes.

⅔ pound (300 g) potatoes
2 ounces (60 g) pork lard
1 onion, thinly sliced
Salt and pepper

Wash the Jerusalem artichokes, cut into halves, brush with butter, and roast for 25 minutes at 300°F (150°C).

7 ounces (200 g) Jerusalem artichokes
1 ounce (30 g) butter

Heat the oil to 300°F (150°C) and deep-fry the sage leaves.

1 cup (200 ml) oil
Sage leaves

TO SERVE:
First place the lamb on a plate, pour sauce over the top, then add the potatoes, Jerusalem artichokes, and fried sage leaves.

LAMB "MOUNTAIN OYSTERS" (TESTICLES)

━━━━━━━━━━

Make a thin cut into the testicle and blanch in boiling water. Transfer to iced water and immediately peel the outer membrane.

Cook in clarified butter, turning and basting, for 10 minutes.

Heat the demi-glace and add the thyme sprigs. Place the testicles in the sauce, cover, and braise for 6 minutes.

Grind the dried mushrooms to a powder in a coffee grinder.

TO SERVE:
Place the testicles on a plate, pour sauce over the top, sprinkle with mushroom powder, fleur de sel, a drizzle of olive oil, and add radish leaves.

4 lamb testicles
3 ounces (80 g) clarified butter (ghee)
1 cup (200 ml) lamb demi-glace
½ cup (100 ml) olive oil
1 bunch thyme
1 ounce (30 g) dried mushrooms
Fleur de sel
Young radish leaves

ACKNOWLEDGMENTS

To Noah Charney, who gave a voice and story to our journeys around Slovenia.

To Matjaž Tančič, who recorded the journey in extraordinary portraits and creative glimpses.

To Manca Jevšček, who took care that all plates are presented in the most beautiful light.

To Žare Kerin, who tied everything together into a wonderful book.

To Marjan Božič, for his meticulous assistance with the design.

To the masters of words, Karina Cunder Reščič, Alenka Bratina, and Simona Škul Tomić.

To Tjaša Gnezda, for lighting the way on our journeys and on Matjaž's portraits.

To excellent cooks who tested all the recipes: Urška Bassin, Karmen Kozjek, and Jana Jovanovska.

All the dishes are served on exquisite plates created by ceramicists Bojana Križanec, Daša Kogoj, and Uršula Kordiš.

Thanks also to Arona d.o.o. for lending the plates.

A big thanks goes to all producers for their generous reception, hospitality, and presentation of their work.

To Hiroshi Ishida, for his preface to the book.

And finally, a special thanks goes to my family, Ema, Nina, and Tomaž, and to my amazing team at JB Restaurant. Thanks to everyone for contributing your effort and ideas for this wonderful book.